CREATE INCOME 2 RETIRE

Start a Business In 8 Easy Steps

By G. Edward Marshall

The Wealth Publishing Group

Teaching Prosperity

"Create Income 2 RETIRE"

Start a Business In 8 Easy Steps

Published By:

The Wealth Publishing Group

Teaching Prosperity

ISBN: 978-0-578-75005-7

To download forms listed herein, go to:
www.CreateIncome2Retire.com

Dedicated to all those who have worked hard all their lives and now want to create the life they have always imagined.

"The world is awash in money! Do you hear what that means? It is awash in money. It is flowing for everyone. It is like Niagara Falls. And most of you are showing up with your teaspoons."

■ *Abraham Hicks*

FOREWARD

G. Edward Marshall has a special gift that entices the reader to not only think about starting a business, but excites the reader to want to get up and be something more in their life. His steps to starting a business are so well laid out chronologically, it's almost as easy as 1-2-3.

He uses everyday language so anyone can understand and follow the steps necessary to enjoy more happiness in their life. Not only has Mr. Marshall done his homework, he has lived the experience of how to create income in retirement.

This book is the answer to all those who think they can never afford to retire or are struggling through retirement financially right now. If I were 25 years younger, I might try it again using his guidelines.

PAUL E. BERNEY
Vice President Sales & Marketing, Retired
Sierra Aluminum Company
Riverside, CA USA

Retirement

The art of pretending leisure, while
income opportunities are all around you.

G. Edward Marshall

CONTENTS

INTRODUCTION

This book is for all those individuals who are at or near retirement and have a soul full of music still left in them. This is for those individuals who want to go out and create something they have always dreamed about accomplishing. Sitting around and watching the grass grow or continually rearranging the furniture in your house soon becomes boring.

You thought you had enough of a nest egg to get you through retirement. Then, required minimum distributions, taxes owed on your retirement money and the high cost of growing older has taken a larger bite out of that nest egg than you expected. This is why you need to read and follow the steps outlined in this book to creating additional income in your life on your schedule.

I use stories and real world experiences to keep you engaged and motivated to become an entrepreneur. I write as if you were sitting next to me and I was teaching you step-by-step how to be in business for yourself. I use everyday language and have omitted the ivory tower platitudes and words so anyone can follow my steps to greater prosperity. I have started and operated eight businesses. Yes, eight! Four have done very well. The other four? Let's just say that I learned a lot of ways how not to run a business. You supply the ***will*** and the ***action*** and I will provide the ***steps*** and ***benefits*** to greater freedom and happiness in your life. Follow me and I will provide you with multiple buckets of income.

■ G. Edward Marshall

en·tre·pre·neur

Noun

Old French, from *entreprendre:* to undertake

Old Definition:

A person who starts a business enterprise and is willing to risk in order to potentially earn money.

New Definition:

Someone who is mad as hell and not going to put up with all the crap anymore!

CHAPTER 1

You're Retired! Yippee! Now What?

"The best way to predict the future is to create it."

—Peter F. Drucker

You've been looking forward to retirement your entire life and now it has finally arrived. Yippee! Now what? Fishing? Camping? Travel? The opportunities are so many. Yet, the first question to ask yourself is, "Do I have enough income to sustain me each month in retirement? For the rest of my life?" Certainly, social security will be there. Is there a pension, IRA, 401(k), cash-value life insurance, annuity or sufficient savings to provide an adequate monthly cash flow?

Most financial advisors will tell you that there is something called the '4% Rule.' If you have $1 Million dollars in savings or investments, you can withdraw 4% per year, that's $40,000.00. Combine that with social security and your life will be wonderful! Oh wait! That's right. You don't have $1 Million dollars. Well, let's see. We can either go back to work (Ah, no! You just came from there) and earn income so part of your social security can be taxed, (Yep! You heard me right) or you can lower your expectations for retirement.

"Oh, but I have a large nest egg in my 401(k) or IRA," you say. That's great! Have you payed taxes on that money yet? Not if your retirement funds are in a government controlled account such as an IRA, 401(k) or public fund program. Uncle Sam has been waiting for his money and he is tired of waiting. Each time you take a withdrawal from one of these government controlled programs, taxes will be deducted BEFORE you get your money. This effectively reduces your lifestyle during retirement. In other words, somewhere between 10%–37% of your nest egg belongs to Uncle Sam. If you live in a state that also charges income taxes, they will have their hand attached to part of your nest egg too! Not fair? I bet the human resources department did not explain that part of the program to you when you signed up for the company retirement plan. If they did, most people just shrugged it off and told themselves, "That's way off in the future." Well, *the future has arrived!* So again, "Now what?"

Many of us want to rest for a while, then go see the kids and grandkids. Next, we would like to travel and see all the places we were too busy to visit while working and raising a family. The prospect of lowering your lifestyle or running out of money too soon is certainly not very appealing. So again, "Now what?"

You could move to an area where the cost of living is lower. It may be that the reason the cost of living is lower is because a lot of people don't want to live there. Maybe the reason the cost of living is lower is due to the fact that it gets too hot, too cold, is prone to earthquakes, hurricanes, tornadoes or large hailstones. Maybe it's due to crime. These are all something to think about.

Another consideration is this: you like where you live. Your friends and social safety net are close by. Your doctor and healthcare facilities are easy to get to. These are all the things you will want to consider BEFORE you retire. So again, "Now what?" Rather than lowering your retirement expectations or facing the possibility of running out of money too soon, **why not supplement your monthly income with a business of your own?**

"Oh no, not me. I just came from there," you say? Again, I ask "now what?" You can lower your expectations, run the risk of running out of money too soon and hope a catastrophic illness does not affect you or your spouse and watch all your hard earned savings go out the window in a hurry. OR, you could start a small business that produces cash-flow each month.

Benefits of Entrepreneurship

It's your turn. It's your time to enjoy greater freedom, flexibility and revenue in life. Owning your own business can give you a reason and a purpose in life. It provides the opportunity to once again use your talents, abilities, skills and the work ethic you've developed over your working years to build YOUR dream and not someone else's dream. There is absolutely no more exhilarating feeling in the world than being in control of your own life and charting your own destiny. That can be a real sense of security. Isn't that what you really want in life? This book will show you how to do it. This is what being a successful business owner can provide. It's the opportunity to improve your life, the chance to be somebody. Pay off your debts; build financial reserves and own assets, not liabilities.

Rather than attempting to live off a pile of cash that is quickly depleting, why not ***'replace income'*** instead? It's much easier, faster and more rewarding.

Owning a business allows you the freedom to do what you want to do in life. The benefits of entrepreneurship can be freedom, increased cash flow, extra tax-deductions and hopefully, more time for family. Owning your own business means you control your destiny and get to work at what you love. Look forward to it. It's exciting and rewarding. Remember, your best investment—*is you*!

The world is rapidly changing. Maybe you are nearing retirement or are already there. I believe that the 'retirement' concept of playing golf all day or sitting in a rocking chair on the front porch watching the grass grow is outdated.

Since many of us are living longer, [1] it has become increasingly difficult to save enough for a 20-30 year retirement in just 40 working years. Think about that for a moment. Let that statement sink into your mind!

By following the principles and steps outlined in this book, I will teach you how to build an asset, (a business) that can become a golden goose that will soon be providing you with golden eggs (extra cash flow) each month. Eventually, you can train others to do the daily work while you go and do more important things in life. You will soon wonder why you ever waited so long to start your own business.

Let's face it. There are really only three ways to earn money in this world. The first way is to own a business. The second way is to own real estate. The third way is to own investments such as stocks, bonds or mutual funds. Either you own them or you worked for someone who did own those items. "Oh, but I was a teacher," you say. That is a business. "I was a firefighter." That's a business. "I worked in an office." You were working for the owner(s). "I was in the military." That too is a business. You see, life is made up of assets and liabilities. Owning your own business is an asset. Assets put money in your pocket. Liabilities, on the other hand, take money out of your pocket. Examples of liabilities are a car, boat, RV and credit cards. Even your house can be a liability until it is paid off in full.

I also believe there is a financial crisis coming to America. Most individuals have not saved enough money to be able to enjoy an affordable retirement.[2] Almost 46% of people today are taking their social security benefits at age 62, the earliest they are allowed under current law to do so.[3] Also, the cost of long-term care is rising and Medicare or Medi-Cal does not cover these costs.[4] Many people are working longer into their *golden years* out of necessity.[5] They have been trying to amass a large mountain of cash to live on in later years. Most people do not save enough. And yes, the markets have taken away much of their wealth in the last few decades. (Ala 2000, 2008 and Coronavirus?) I have met many schoolteachers who have returned to teaching because they said they were "just bored." Yeah! Right!

If you're looking for the short cut to getting rich quick, this is not the guide for you. In fact, there is no such book! In 5 – 10 years, how old will you be? You'll be the same age whether you are rich or poor. How about being richer than you are today? And yes, if you wait, you WILL be poorer. With the rising costs of health care, energy and inflation, EVERYTHING is going to be more expensive in the future.[6] You and I have been around long enough to remember 35-cents per gallon gasoline and the 5-cent jelly donut. They no longer exist. The rising cost of living has increased these prices significantly. Yet, personal incomes have not kept pace with the inflationary prices we now pay and will pay in the future.[7]

Don't put your hopes and dreams in someone else's pocket. Build your own pocket and then work at making your pocket bigger so there is room enough for family and friends to succeed with you. I believe that is the true definition of a great entrepreneur.

Also, have you noticed that what you buy is becoming more expensive? It now takes more dollars to buy the same thing you bought just 5-10 years ago.[8] In 1967, a cool $1 million dollars would have bought you a lot. Fast forward 50 years and you would need $7.4 million dollars to purchase that same lifestyle. Even if you had $1 million dollars just 20 years ago, you would require $1.5 million dollars in 2017 to equal the buying power of 1997.[9] Incomes are not keeping up with our shrinking dollars. This is all the more reason to begin a cash flow business that you own and control.

As you start a business of your own, it will require a different mindset. Yes, there are headaches, but the opportunities to get ahead are so much more profitable. I am going to teach you how to start and operate your own cash flow enterprise with just an idea and a small amount of capital to begin. Your life can soon be exhilarating again. Are you ready? Turn the page and let's get started!

[1] https://www.statnews.com/2017/02/14/living-longer-without-better-aging/

[2] https://www.usatoday.com/story/money/personalfinance/retirement/2017/03/03/10-statistics-that-prove-baby-boomers-are-in-big-trouble/98526764/

[3] https://www.fool.com/retirement/2017/05/22/should-the-average-american-take-social-security-a.aspx

[4] https://www.medicare.gov/coverage/long-term-care.html

[5] http://www.pewresearch.org/fact-tank/2016/06/20/more-older-americans-are-working-and-working-more-than-they-used-to/

[6] http://www.nytimes.com/books/first/s/stanley-millionaire.html

[7] http://www.pewresearch.org/fact-tank/2014/10/09/for-most-workers-real-wages-have-barely-budged-for-decades/

[8] http://www.pewtrusts.org/en/about/news-room/press-releases/2015/11/18/pew-finds-american-families-ill-equipped-for-financial- emergencies

[9] The Press-Enterprise pg.4, August 6, 2017

CHAPTER 2

Don't Be Brain Dead

■ **Sandy Botkin CPA, Esq.**

This is the shortest chapter in the book. It may also be one of the most important chapters. You may be thinking, "I will just go get a job part-time to supplement my retirement income" or you may decide to tell your spouse, "Honey, it's time to get a job." These thoughts may be the worst idea you ever had. Why do I say that? Please put this book down and go on-line and view the following video. It may be the most profitable eight minutes of your life.

Go ahead! Watch the video, then come back and let's get your business party started! The video is called ***"2013 Tax Secrets by Sandy Botkin" at*** www.google.com. The numbers may be a little different in today's world, but the concept is the same. Or on-line at https://www.youtube.com/watch?v=TNPC7_FiE-g

Go! Now!

Did you view the video? I have always hated statistics, but they provide us with a clear picture of reality. A recent news article showed that 48% of American workers retired earlier than expected. The unemployment rate of workers over age 55 was 2.6% in January 2020. By April 2020, that figure had jumped to 13.6% due to the Coronavirus Pandemic. Many of these workers will never find full-time employment again.[1] Also, many retirees are finding they are spending more on healthcare related expenses than they had planned.[2] This, of course, has the effect of reducing available income for living expenses during retirement.

TD Ameritrade recently conducted a study and found that health and employment shifts are the most common triggers for early retirement.[3]

Here are the numbers:

38% Health Issues
22% Laid off / Asked to leave (What's the difference?)
11% Caregiving Responsibilities
5% Change in financial situation i.e. Gain/loss [3]

Another eye-popping survey showed that 7 in 10 retirees say overall lifestyle in retirement is less than expected. Most plan to cut back during retirement in anticipation of longevity.[4]

I'm not letting a lack of income stop me from enjoying possibly the best years of my life. If you haven't already, watch the video, then turn the page and let's start your journey of earning cash-flow and building an asset that may outlive you.

1 Maurice Backman The Motley Fool, Fox Business News May 16, 2020

2 Shawn M. Carter Fox Business News May 22, 2020

3 The Harris Poll on behalf of TD Ameritrade; n=733 (retirees); n=367 (retired earlier) Retirement Confidence Survey 2020

4 2020 Retirement Confidence Survey: Employee Benefits Research Institute (EBRI)

CHAPTER 3

Excuses, Excuses!

"Our greatest fear should not be of failure, but of succeeding at things in life that don't really matter."

— Francis Chan

This is one of my favorite chapters in this book. When I begin telling people the benefits of starting a business of their own for extra cash-flow, I am immediately introduced to all the reasons why they can't do it. As Jean Chatzky, a women's financial coach has stated, "You can either make money or you can make excuses, but not both."

Let's start with the most important ingredient to success: Belief in yourself. This is akin to faith. Having faith in your own abilities. Faith that you can do this and be successful, no matter how long it takes. Next comes planning, discipline, perseverance and of course work. Because you are working for yourself, you can enjoy having fun doing it. Isn't that the kind of life you would like to lead? Why not create a life you do not need a vacation from?

On the road to success, your *'will'* to succeed needs to be larger than the obstacles you will encounter along the way. The obstacles are the things you see when you take your eyes off the road of your priorities. And always remember, on the road to success, there are no shortcuts.

Let's first define success. What is success to you? It is different for every one of us. To some it may be money and fame. To another person, it may be the freedom to be creative and follow your dreams.

Still, others just want to be happy at what they do in life and enjoy the ride. I have personally found success to be the ability to create for myself the life I have imagined without another person telling me what I have to do or when to do it.

In the paragraphs that follow, I would like to introduce you to some people who followed their dream and did not give excuses. They had faith in themselves to follow their passion in life and would not let anything stand in their way.

Excuses

I'm too old

Harland D. Sanders of Kentucky Fried Chicken (KFC) fame was born in 1890. He grew up in a poor family in Indiana. His father died when he was 7 years old. His mother went to work in a tomato cannery and was gone for days at a time. This left Harland to care and cook for his two siblings. His mother later remarried and Harland could not get along with his stepfather. At age thirteen, he left home to live with relatives. Throughout his life, Harland Sanders had an array of jobs working for the railroads, selling insurance and practicing law until he had a brawl in the courtroom with his own client. In 1930, Harland was approached by a large oil company and was offered a gasoline station, rent free, if he would pay a royalty on each gallon of gasoline sold. While operating his station, Sanders began to serve chicken dishes and other meals from his living quarters. He eventually opened a small restaurant nearby. During this time, it was reported that Sanders was involved in a shootout with a local competitor after having repainted a sign directing traffic to Sanders gas station.

Sanders was commissioned as a Kentucky colonel in 1935 by the Kentucky governor whom he had befriended. The title 'colonel' was honorary.

He began selling fried chicken from his roadside restaurant in North Corbin, Kentucky, during the Great Depression. During that time Sanders developed his "secret recipe" and his patented method of cooking chicken in a pressure fryer. In 1952 at the age of 65, when most people are looking at slowing down and retiring, Colonel Harland D. Sanders began Kentucky Fried Chicken. He went door-to-door offering to cook his chicken in the restaurant for each prospective franchisee. The first restaurant owner to accept his 'recipe' was in South Salt Lake City, Utah. In the first year, the Salt Lake City's restaurant tripled their income with 75% of the new revenue coming from sales of the colonel's fried chicken. By the time of Colonel Sander's death in June 1980, there were over 6,000 KFC restaurants in 48 countries. Not bad for someone whom others would say he was 'too old.'

I'm afraid

It's natural to feel that way. Join the club. Fear is part of everyone's personality. It is a natural trait of each one of us who still has a heartbeat. Fear is the opposite of enthusiasm. Fear feeds depression and pessimism. Enthusiasm feeds health, wealth and happiness. Faith and fear cannot coexist. Fear is also one of the great motivating forces of the world. Many of us went to college to earn a degree because we feared not being able to get a good job. We saved for retirement so we could work into our old age by choice and not of necessity. Being afraid can also cripple, debilitate and even destroy us. Let me give you an example.

Harry L. Wilson wrote a story back in 1912. It's about a young man named ***Bunker Bean***.

Bunker Bean was orphaned when he was just a child. No one wanted him, so he roamed the world in rags hiding from the things that scared him. He was afraid of policemen, riding (or falling) in elevators, afraid of situations, things, the future, even himself on occasion. In essence, he was full of fears. Because he lived his life this way, others would often make fun of him thereby confirming his fears.

Bunker Bean lived in the attic of a cheap boarding house. One day, a false fortuneteller moved into the boarding house and began to tell Bunker Bean about the great karmic cycles that existed in the universe. He owned a book on reincarnation and explained that each person went through many lives during their existence. Bunker's new friend explained that in exchange for some of Bunker Bean's money, he could discover who Bunker Bean might have been in a previous life. After considerable time and prodding, Bunker Bean finally agreed to give this false fortuneteller some of his money. As the false fortuneteller gazed into his crystal ball, the fortuneteller became very excited and could not believe what he saw. This fortuneteller explained that in a previous life, he, Bunker Bean, was the great Napoleon Bonaparte. Back then, Bunker Bean was not afraid of policemen. In fact, all of Europe trembled at his name. Bunker Bean was shocked! How could this be? What happened? Bunker Bean's friend explained that the universe goes through vast karmic cycles and that now this cycle was on the ascendancy and soon, Bunker Bean would be a successful person again.

With this newfound knowledge, Bunker Bean went back upstairs to his attic hideaway. He stood and studied himself in his old, rusty mirror. Suddenly, he realized that indeed, there *was* some resemblance. He soon went to the local library and read every book he could find about Napoleon. He even found a picture in an old magazine of Napoleon sitting on his white horse overlooking a precipice waving his sword above his head urging his troops on to victory. Bunker Bean taped this picture to his mirror and looked at it as often as he could through the glare of the single light bulb hanging from the attic ceiling. Bunker Bean thought that if there were no more wars to conquer, he would overcome his fears and conquer the business world.

Slowly, Bunker Bean began to think and act *'as if'* he were Napoleon. He began thinking positive thoughts about himself and the future. This resulted in Bunker Bean appearing happier and more outgoing in his demeanor. His boss at work noticed this change and gave Bunker Bean additional responsibilities. Along with these additional responsibilities, of course, came more money.

One day as Bunker Bean was working, the thought occurred to him. "Who was I before I was Napoleon?" That evening, Bunker Bean once again sat down with his fortuneteller friend and asked him to once again look into his crystal ball and find out who he was in a life previous to being Napoleon. Once again, as money was exchanged, Bunker Bean's friend did not disappoint.

"Why Bunker," said his friend. "You were Ramses, the greatest pharaoh that ever ruled in Egypt. The people loved you." With this newfound knowledge, Bunker Bean once again studied himself in the mirror. He decided to act with majesty, empathy and concern for others. He even went to a local tailor and had a suit made for him that made him look taller. Again, Bunker Bean's employer noticed the differences coming over Bunker Bean and promoted him several times until Bunker Bean was an important person in his company.

Then, one day, Bunker Bean made a tragic discovery. He learned that his fortune telling friend was a fraud. That this supposed friend had taken Bunker Bean's money and filled his head with stories. But a strange thing happened. While Bunker Bean was listening to this charlatan, Bunker Bean was filled with positive and uplifting thoughts of success and confidence. He had learned new, successful habits. Since no one other than his fallen friend knew that Bunker Bean believed he was Napoleon and Ramses, he decided to continue with his positive self-image. He was no longer afraid of policemen, elevators, the future or *things.* Eventually, Bunker Bean became a wonderful success in his life.

I have always enjoyed this story. By starting a business of your own, you too have the potential to enjoy greater success. Don't let fear of the unknown get the better of you. That's why I am here. I will guide you through every step of starting a business. Just follow my steps and let's have some fun.

I don't have a degree

Really? You want me to go there? In today's modern world, even those of us who are at or near retirement do not need a 'degree' to start a business. What we need is an example. Someone who has already started a business or businesses. I have started eight businesses in my lifetime. Four have done very well. The other four? Let's just say that I learned what not to do from those other experiences. And that is exactly what I received. Experience. An education in how to prepare better and understand what works and what does not. Still need convincing? Here is a partial list of those who either never went to college and received a degree or dropped out before they graduated. Bill Gates of Microsoft. Steve Jobs of Apple Computer. Mark Zuckerberg, founder of Facebook. Larry Ellison is the founder of Oracle Software. He started with $1,200.00 of his own money. He is now worth billion$. Jack Dorsey started Twitter which even presidents and heads of state use to communicate their ideas and opinions worldwide. Rachel Ray is a television personality and author of many books. She has a college degree, but not a culinary degree. John Mackey is the CEO of Whole Foods Market, a large grocery retailer. Russell Simmons is chairman and CEO of Rush Communications, co-founded the hip-hop music label Def Jam Recordings and created the clothing fashion line Phat Farm and many others. Follow me and I will provide you with an honorary degree in Entrepreneurship. No previous experience needed.

It takes luck to succeed in business

It has been said that, "The smarter and harder I work, the luckier I get." That has been my experience throughout life. I'm sure you have found that to be true in your life as well. If you want to succeed in business, look for someone who has traveled that road and do what they did. Remember, 'luck' is when preparation meets opportunity. I will show you how, step-by-step, in the next few chapters. Follow me.

I don't know what to do or where to start

Start where you are and let's do this together. Follow my lead and you will be miles ahead in your attempt than trying to do it all on your own. That's why you have me. A serial entrepreneur.

I don't have any money

Great! You don't owe anybody. I started my first company with $700.00. Of that amount, $500 was borrowed. I'll show you how to find the money in Step 4.

I'm not good at anything

Wrong. We all have talents, skills and abilities we can use to start a business. Sit down in a quiet location, close the door and answer honestly the following questions. Don't worry, you are going to be the only person that will see these answers.

1. What have other people told me I am good at doing?
2. If money was not a problem, what would I do to make me happy?
3. What is my purpose in life?
4. Where have I been successful in the past?
5. What are my strengths?

6. What specifically does God (or the Universe) want me to do?
7. If I knew I only had five years to live, what would I absolutely, positively have to accomplish for my life to have been meaningful?

Now, gather your answers. Take the top three ideas in each question and develop a 'mission statement' for yourself.

I don't have the right skills

What skills did you perform during your working years? We are all good at doing something. Make a list of what you did well in your previous profession.

Next, make a list of the skills you would like to acquire for the next 15-20 years.

I Don't Have the Right contacts

Do you have a neighbor? With whom did you work with during your working years? Do you talk to the checker at the grocery store? How about the dry cleaner? Your mechanic? Unless you live in the Gobi desert, potential contacts are all around you. I will show you how to turn them into the 'right' contacts.

I don't live in the right city

Women all over India are making a living sewing clothing, making handicrafts and buying and reselling food items. You live in the land of opportunity. It is all around you. See it? Travel to any city in America and you will see the same chain stores, franchises and brands you see in your own city. You and I can earn money wherever we live.

I don't have any equipment/tools

Let's get creative together. I'll teach you how to find what you need in Step 1.

I don't have an office

Start in a spare bedroom or at the kitchen table. Michael Dell started his computer empire from his school dorm. Hewlitt-Packard and Apple Computer both started in a garage. I started my first business with a Masonite door set on top of two wooden sawhorses in a spare bedroom. Eventually, I moved to an office inside a warehouse.

I don't have time

You're retired! You will find the time if you schedule it. Your success is in direct proportion to where you direct your time and resources. Don't succeed at things that don't really matter! Let's make positive things happen in your life.

I don't feel good

My experience is that if you set a goal to pursue a purpose that excites you, your energy level will increase. You will find that if you spend time pursuing your passion, you will forget your aches and pains. I believe that soon, you will find a new vigor and outlook on life you never imagined before. Look forward to it. It's exhilarating.

These are just a few of the excuses I have heard from others. You and I can make excuses or we can make money. Remember that a determined purpose cannot be stopped or hindered. Your thoughts will make or break you. Thoughts of prosperity attract while thoughts of poverty repel. It's all an inside job! Believing in yourself is all that matters. Now! Let's get on with *your* success story!

I bargained with life for a penny,
Only to find dismayed
That anything I had asked of life,
Life would have willingly paid.

— Jessie B. Rittenhouse

CHAPTER 4

Peter, Paul & Money

"Where Have All the Flowers Gone?"

— Song by Peter, Paul and Mary, 1962

We often hear the phrase "robbing Peter to pay Paul." The question is really, "How much does Paul really need every month to survive?" Before you start your business, you will need to know exactly how much money it takes to run your household each month. This is your financial starting point. To the best of your knowledge, fill in all the blanks below that apply to you to determine what it actually costs you to live each month.

EXPENSES	Monthly Payment
Bank Charges	
Cable TV	
Cell Phone	
Charity	
Clothing	
Credit Card Totals	
Entertainment	
Gasoline	
Groceries	
House Payment 1st	
House Payment 2nd	
HELOC	
House Insurance	

Internet	
401k, etc.	
Life Insurance	
Medical Expense	
Dental Expense	
Postage	
Savings	
Subscriptions	
House Phone	
Car Insurance	
Car Maintenance	
Vehicle Pmt. #1	
Vehicle Pmt. #2	
Other:	
Other:	
Other:	
Electric	
Water	
Gas	
Trash/Sewer	
Total Mo. Expenses	

Was this a surprise to you? Most people never really sit down and figure out how much it costs to run their home. Are there some areas in your budget that you can go without, at least for a while? Maybe it's time for the "B" word. You know. Budget! ***A budget is where you tell your money where to go instead of it telling you where it went.*** This is part of how wealth is built, but that's a subject for another book. Right now, you need to know how much money you need to earn each month just to pay your household bills. In addition to this, when you go full time in your new business, you will also add in your monthly business expenses to come up with a total monthly cash flow to finance both your household and business.

Remember. We are doing our homework here so that when you implement your business venture, the launch will go smoother, faster and with fewer headaches. Then, you will know how much it takes to pay the bills each month. This is where knowledge becomes power.

Marshall's Rule #1

When you can earn enough money to support yourself for six consecutive months in your new venture, it's time to make a decision about your full-time job, if you are still working.

CHAPTER 5

Entrepreneurship, Social Security And Taxation

"When the legislature is in session, no man's wallet is safe."

— Mark Twain

One of my favorite reasons for being self-employed is paying less taxes than if I were an employee. If you are an employee, Uncle Sam, also known as the Internal Revenue Service, is your 50/50 business partner. As an employee, you probably pay a higher tax percentage than many company owners.

Please be aware that there are two tax systems in America. As mentioned in the previous video, there is one tax system for employees and another tax system for business owners. As I said, business owners typically pay less in taxes as a percentage than an employee. This can potentially put more money in your pocket. This is again one of my favorite reasons why I like being in business for myself.

As an employee, you worked hard for your money. Didn't you? You were in essence renting out your time and efforts to your employer. At the end of each pay period, you earned a certain amount of money. This was your *'gross'* pay. Your employer then deducted your payroll taxes according to federal tax rules and sent your tax money to the IRS. The difference was your *'net'* pay. This is what you took home and lived on until your next paycheck. This is how the majority of Americans receive their payroll income each month.

As a business owner, the current tax laws are much more favorable. As a sole proprietor for example, you also work hard for your money. But this time, you are working for yourself, not your employer. Feels good, right? Oh, but it gets better! You see, each month, your business generates a certain amount of income. This is called *'gross receipts.'* This is the total amount of money people have paid to you for your product or service. Now comes the fun part!

From your *'gross receipts,'* the IRS allows you to deduct the expenses incurred to provide your product or service. Expenses can include such things as gasoline, vehicle payments, inventory items, business insurance, business lunch meetings, computers, printer ink, etc. Once you have deducted all your expenses from your *'gross receipts,'* the smaller number is what you pay your taxes on. Let's look at an example.

Mike is in the plumbing business. Mary calls Mike and says her kitchen sink is clogged. Mike goes out to her house and finds that the tree roots in her front yard have grown into her sewer line and clogged the pipes. Mike unclogs the sewer line from the house to the street at Mary's house. She pays Mike $100.00 for this service.

Mike does this type of service 1,000 times during the year and earns gross receipts of $100,000.00. ($100 X 1,000 = $100,000) If you were an employee earning this $100,000.00, your employer would have deducted your payroll taxes and sent you your net pay. This *'net'* pay is what you would live on for the remainder of the year.

Since Mike is a sole proprietor, Mike gets to deduct his business expenses from his *'gross receipts'* **before** estimating what taxes he will be required to pay. As was mentioned previously, he can deduct expenses such as his advertising, truck payment, vehicle insurance, business liability insurance, parts, checking account fees, legal and accounting fees, office supplies, printing costs, internet, utilities, office rent, mileage or gasoline and much more. After deducting these business expenses from his *'gross receipts'*, Mike pays taxes on the smaller number.

Because Mike is paying taxes on the smaller number, he gets to keep ***more*** of his hard earned money. Wouldn't you like to do the same? If Mike is working from his home, he may also claim a portion of his rent or house payment and utility payments as a legitimate tax deduction. This is known as the 'home office deduction.' Mike can even deduct his mileage as a tax-deduction. This **legal** tax system can put more money in your pocket.

MIKE'S DISCOUNT PLUMBING SERVICE

Example:

Gross Annual Receipts	$100,000
Advertising	
Bank Fees	
Business Insurance	
Cell Phones	
Charity	
Clothing	
Continuing Education	
Entertainment	

Gasoline
Gifts Given
Health Insurance
Internet
License Fees
Office Supplies
Office Equipment
Postage
Printing
Subscriptions
Telephones
Vehicle Payments
Vehicle Insurance
Vehicle Maintenance

Minus Annual Deductions	**-$50,000**
* Not a complete list	________
Taxable Annual Income	$50,000

WARNING: As an employee, your employer deducted your taxes and sent the taxes to the appropriate government agency. As an entrepreneur, YOU are responsible for submitting your tax payments on a quarterly basis. Remember to pay your taxes on time. If you don't, the IRS will be more than willing to tack on additional penalties and interest. A good certified public accountant (CPA) can help you stay on the right side of the tax laws.

Following is a partial list of available tax deductions for business owners.

Advertising
Alarm Systems
Bank Fees
Business Cards
Business Bond
Business Brochures

Business Insurance
Business License
Business Lunches
Business Training
Cell Phone
Checking Account Fees
Computer
Computer Repair
Computer Software
Copy Machine
Charity
Clothing
Consulting Fees
Continuing Education
Desk
Dry Cleaning
Fax Machine
Filing Cabinet
Gasoline
Gifts Given
Health Insurance
Inkjet Cartridges
Internet
Inventory Supplies
Legal Fees
Liability Insurance
License Fees
Mortgage Payment[1]
Office Cleaning
Office Rent
Office Supplies
Office Equipment
Office Furniture
Office Utilities
Paper
Payroll
Postage
Printing
Printer
Printing Supplies
Parts
Rent Payment[1]
Shipping Charges
Stamps
Subscriptions
Telephone
Telephone System
Thank You Cards
Toll Lanes
Tools
Uniforms
Utilities[1]
Vehicle Payment
Vehicle Insurance
Vehicle Maintenance
Vehicle Mileage
Website Fees

These deductions **MUST** be for a legitimate business purpose. If you are still working and have yet to retire, you can use the same principles Mike used in his plumbing business to earn extra income and receive extra tax deductions. These extra tax deductions 'may' offset the payroll taxes you are required to pay as an employee. This 'extra' money you now have can be used to pay down credit cards, pay-off your mortgage faster or enhance the quality of your life.

Social Security & Taxes

Many people are under the misconception that taxes are a small part of their budget and they do not pay that much in taxes. This is not true. I believe that we all pay up to fifty percent of our income in taxes in one form or another. Every business is taxed on the raw materials they use to manufacture a product. These taxes are passed along in the price we pay for everything. Of course, some jurisdictions allow products to be purchased on a tax-deferred basis if they are to be used in manufacturing or producing a final product. When the item is sold, that is when taxes will be assessed at a higher amount.

Think about how you go about your daily routine. When you wake up and turn on the lights, you pay a utility tax. When the shower goes on, the water is taxed. The gas or electricity to heat the water is taxed. When you make your morning coffee, again, the water, gas or electricity is taxed. When you flush the toilet, you are again being taxed. Get in your car. Did you pay a tax (Oops!) a 'fee' for your license and registration? How about when you last filled the gas tank, didn't you pay taxes on each gallon of gasoline? When your old tires are discarded, you pay a 'disposal tax.' While talking on your cell phone, you are being taxed. Drive-thru food today? You were taxed. Did you deduct money from your payroll check to go to your 401(k)? It will be taxed when you withdraw the money in retirement. What about the taxes paid from your full or part-time employment check? If Medicaid or Medi-Cal is paying for your long-term care expenses, your local jurisdiction may require your estate to reimburse the state coffers for any benefits you or your spouse received following your demise.

In other words, ***when you earn it, they tax it. When you spend it, they tax it. When you save it, they tax it. When you die, they tax it.*** Even the insurance policy premium you pay each month for your house, car or life contains a state premium tax.

If you are currently receiving Social Security benefits, up to 85% of your benefit can be taxed![2] No, that was not a misprint.

If you are single or married and receive no other income other than Social Security benefits, your benefits are not taxed. You're probably also poor. If you have reached full retirement age and file as a single filer and earn in excess of $25,000 or married filing jointly and earn in excess of $32,000 per year, your Social Security benefits can be taxed up to 50%.[2]

If you have reached full retirement age and file as a single filer and earn in excess of $34,000 or are married filing jointly and earn in excess of $44,000 per year, your Social Security benefits can be taxed up to 85%. [2]

Think that is all? Wait! There's more. If you are below your full retirement age and receiving Social Security benefits and earning in excess of $18,240 per year, $1.00 of benefits are withheld for every $2.00 of earnings above the limit. These benefits are withheld each month until the month you reach your full retirement age.[2]

This why I say that we all pay *up to fifty percent of our income* in taxes in one form or another. So, what is to be done about this egregious amount of money we pay each month? The answer is simple. Start a business and enjoy all the tax laws that benefit small business owners that you learned in the video in Chapter 2.

Turn items you usually purchase into tax-deductions. By simply using 'legal' tax laws, you can keep more of your hard earned money and lower you tax burden.

"But wait!" You may be asking, "If I earn additional money, won't I be paying more in taxes?" The simple answer is, 'yes.' But, you won't be broke either.

I have found that the extra cash I earn far outweighs any extra taxes I am required to pay. The 'extra' cash I earn provides me with an enhanced lifestyle while using 'legal' tax strategies to limit my tax exposure.

When I first started in business for myself, I was paying up to $8,000.00 or more in annual income taxes. When I learned these concepts and paid a CPA to mitigate my tax burden, I lowered my taxes *by almost half*. Yes, I paid more to a CPA for tax preparation than if I did my own taxes, but saved thousands in the process. It was all worth it! I recommend using a banking software program such as Quicken Deluxe®[6] to track your income and expenses. At the end of each month, you can print a report and track where your money went and keep track of legal tax deductions. At the end of the year, you can again print an annual report and provide this to your tax professional in order to 'legally' deduct your allowed expenses. Always consult with a qualified tax professional to help you 'legally' avoid paying unnecessary taxes.

The News Less Reported

A recent survey by the *Insured Retirement Institute* [4] showed that 47% of baby-boomers have already retired. Of the total number of baby-boomers alive today, it is estimated that at least 45% have zero savings and cannot afford to retire. If you find yourself in this situation, my suggestion is to keep working until age 70 ***and then*** claim your social security benefits. This will provide the maximum benefits you are entitled to for the remainder of your life. In the meantime, begin a part-time business on the side so that when you do retire, you will have an established cash-flow enterprise already up and running. Yes, it's work. But, the rewards are so worth it.

Tax Deductions for Seniors[5]

I have included the following list for informational purposes only. These possible deductions are available to anyone who qualifies and are not reserved just for business owners. These are out-of-pocket expenses and can be deductible if not covered by Medicare or other insurance. [2]

- Hospitalization
- Doctors / Visits
- Dental Care
- Co-pays
- Weight Loss[3]
- Alcohol Treatment[3]
- Psychiatrists
- Podiatrists
- Prescriptions
- Eyeglasses
- Smoking Cessation [3]
- Medical Mileage

Premiums for qualified long-term care insurance and health insurance are not paid for with pre-tax dollars. Also, if your doctor places you under special medical care, you may be able to deduct your costs for housing, food, clothing, transportation and certain home modifications.

Are you starting to see the benefits of entrepreneurship? You are building the *'Golden Goose'* that can pay you *'Golden Eggs'* each month.

Marshall's Rule #2

"Entrepreneurship can be the Golden Goose that produces your Golden Eggs."

[1] If you are working from your home, only a portion of these expenses may be deducted.

[2] https://www.ssa.gov/planners/taxes.html

[3] May be deductible if part of a treatment plan for a specific disease

[4] https://www.cnbc.com/2019/04/09/baby-boomers-face-retirement-crisis-little-savings-high-health-costs-and-unrealistic-expectations.html

[5] Medical Expense Tax Deduction: Key Characteristics by State. AARP Public Policy Institute, IRS.Gov. In 2019 and beyond, medical expenses may be deductible if more than 10% of AGI

[6] We do not endorse nor have any affiliation with Quicken®

CHAPTER 6

Wait! I'm Not Finished Taking Your Money

– Uncle Sam

As mentioned previously, if you are an employee, Uncle Sam is your 50/50 joint partner with the income you earn. Why do I say that? Under the current tax system, most Americans can pay up to 50% of their income in taxes. I say this because if you factor in not only federal taxes, (state taxes?) vehicle registration fees, (taxes) gasoline taxes, utility taxes, property taxes, sales taxes and other 'fees,' it accumulates to a large dollar amount 'hemorrhaging' from your pocket. This is why so many people are finding it more and more difficult to make ends meet in today's economy.[1]

Below is a partial list of taxes many hard working Americans (and retirees) pay without ever realizing the extent of how much they really pay in taxes.

Accounts Receivable Tax
Building Permit Tax
Driver's License Tax
Cigarette Tax
Corporate Income Tax
Dog License Tax
Federal Income Tax
Federal Unemployment Tax (FUTA)

Fishing License Tax
Food License Tax
Fuel Permit Tax
Gasoline Tax
Hunting License Tax
Inheritance Tax
Inventory Tax
IRS Interest Charges (tax on top of tax),
IRS Penalties (tax on top of tax),
Liquor Tax,
Lumber Tax
Luxury Tax,
Marriage License Tax,
Medicare Tax,
Paint Recycling Tax
Property Tax,
Real Estate Tax,
Recreational Vehicle Tax,
Road Usage Tax (Truckers),
Service Charge Taxes,
Social Security Tax,
Sales Taxes,
School Tax,
Soda Bottle tax
State Income Tax,
State Unemployment Tax (SUTA),
Telephone Federal Excise Tax,
Telephone Federal Universal Service Tax,
Telephone Federal, State and Local
Surcharge Tax,

Telephone Minimum Usage Surcharge Tax,
Telephone Recurring and Non-recurring
Charges Tax,
Telephone State and Local Tax,
Telephone Usage Charge Tax,
Utility Tax,
Vehicle License Registration Tax,
Vehicle Sales Tax,
Watercraft Registration Tax,
Water Bottle Recycle Tax
Well Permit Tax,
Workers Compensation Tax.

You may be thinking, "I don't pay many of these taxes myself." Every business passes along its costs, including taxes paid by the business, to the retail price of everything you and I purchase. In the end, the consumer pays for everything.

Not one of these taxes existed 100 years ago and there was prosperity, absolutely no national debt, the largest middle class in the world and Mom stayed home to raise the kids.

[1] https://www.marketwatch.com/story/half-of-americans-are-just-one-paycheck-away-from-financial-disaster-2019-05-16

CHAPTER 7

Step 1: The Idea

"Thinking is the hardest work there is.
That is why so few people engage in it."
—Henry Ford

Now that you've decided to be your own boss, the first step is to decide what you are going to do for other people that will cause them to pay you for your service, product or idea. If you want to be a business owner, but you are not sure what to do or you would like someone to hold your hand along the way, choose a mentor, a franchise or a relationship marketing organization. (Amway, Avon, etc.)

When I started my first enterprise, I wanted to earn more money and have more freedom. I began with something I already knew. It was a service business. I knew my craft and I enjoyed dealing with people. It's much easier to begin with something you already know how to do. Here's a secret: Do something you love to do. Something you have a passion for doing. If you're going to work, why not work at something you enjoy and get paid to do it.

When deciding what kind of business to get into, first look inward. Ask yourself questions such as:

- What am I good at doing?
- What talents or abilities have I acquired over the years?

- What service can I perform or knowledge can I impart that people would be willing to pay for?
- Am I a people person?

Over the years, we all have learned how to do something well. Plumbing, house framing, electrical work, sewing, quilting, computer repair and insurance are good examples. Having experience in more than one field opens up additional opportunities to earn extra income. Start with what you know.

If you want to be in business for yourself, but you are still drawing a blank about which direction to go, you will find below a list of possible businesses you could start to stimulate your thinking.

Partial List of Possible Start-Up Businesses

3-D Printer Service
Accountant
Adult Daycare
Advertising
Air Conditioning
Antique Dealer
Appraiser
Arborist
Architect
Artist/Artist Supply
Auctioneer
Audio/Visual Service
Auditor
Auto Detail
Auto Repair
Bakery
Beauty Salon/Supply
Beverage Distributor
Bodyguard Service
Candy Maker/Store
Carpenter
Carpet/Flooring
Carpet Cleaning
Catering Service
Check Cashing
Childcare/After School
Clothing Store Owner
Coffee Delivery Service
Computer Consultant
Computer Repair
Contract Writer
Consultant
Delivery Service
Designer

Diesel Repair
Direct Mail Service
Donut Store
Drywall Repair
Electrician
Employment Agency
Engineer
Errand Service
Farmer
Farm Equipment Sales
Flood/Fire Repair
Florist
Foreclosures
Franchise Owner
Fund Raiser
General Contracting
Granite Countertops
Graphic Design
Grocery Delivery
Handyman
Health Care Consulting
Heating & Cooling
Home Healthcare
Home Inspection
House Cleaning
House Sitter
Import-Export
Insurance Agent
Interior Decorator
Janitorial Service
Janitorial Supply
Jewelry Sales/Repair
Laundromat
Landscaping
Lawn Care
Lawn Fertilizing
Lecturer
Limousine Service
Machinist
Magnetic Signs
Management Consultant
Marketing Service
Mobile Home Repair
Mobile Income Tax
Music Teacher
Networks Specialist
Newsletter Writer
Non-Emergency
Medical Transportation
Notary
Office Machines
Painting
Party Planner
Pest Control
Pet Sitting
Petting Zoo
Photographer
Pilot Car Service
Pizza Restaurant
Plumbing

- Pool Cleaning
- Pool Repair
- Pooper Scooper
- PO Box Store
- Pressure Washing
- Printing Service
- Private Tutor
- Property Manager
- Public Relations
- Publisher
- Real Estate Agent
- Roofing Contracting
- Sales Rep
- Salvage/Scrap Metal
- Sand Blasting
- Sandwich/Deli Store
- Santa Claus
- Screen Printing
- Screen Repair Service
- Security Service
- Service Station Owner
- Ship/Boat Repair/Sales
- Sign Maker/Service
- Smart Phone Tutor
- Tax Preparer
- Tool Supply
- Travel Agency
- Tree Trimming
- Used Car Sales
- Water Delivery Service
- Wedding Planner
- Welding Contracting
- Wholesale Distributor
- Window/Glass Repair
- Window Washing
- Yard Clean Up

Naturally, because many of us are not physically able to perform many of these business, we can still use our knowledge and management skills and hire others to perform the work for us.

If you still cannot find something you think you might enjoy doing and could possibly get paid for doing it, find an old telephone book. You know, one of those books no one uses anymore except for maybe a doorstop? Open the yellow pages and look at the index. Run your finger down the pages and notice all the services and businesses listed. Choose a field or career that may be of interest to you. Make a list and then seriously place a number from 1 to 3 next to each possibility. Number 1 means very interested, number 2 for somewhat interested and number 3 for a maybe. Make a list of all of those possibilities you have marked with the number 1. These are the areas you will ponder over first. Could those business ideas you have marked with a number 2 or number 3 be incorporated with your number 1 ideas?

Once you have decided which path you will embark upon, pause and give your decision a few days to settle and percolate in your subconscious. Listen to your subconscious. At some point in the near future, your mind will provide you with additional items to consider. You may wake up in the middle of the night or be watching a television show when your subconscious mind will say, "Ok. Here's your answer."

Once you have decided what service or product you will be providing, research what it's going to take to start a business performing each of these choices. As mentioned earlier, if your start up is something you already know, then you most likely know what you will need to do to open your doors.

With all that having been said, it's time to do your homework. This is one of the most important parts of a business start-up. It's called the 'planning and research' stage. This is where you gather the necessary information to make an intelligent and wise decision.

- How long will it take to get started?
- How much money will you need to start?
- Will you begin from your home or will you need an office or warehouse?
- Are there any special licenses or permits you will need?

First, make a list of all the equipment, supplies and inventory you will need to start. Then, write down the cost of each item. Part of the process of starting your own business is to determine how much it is going to cost you to begin and what kind of inventory, if any, are you going to need? Every business is different. Some businesses require few items at start up and others will need more to get started.

Ask yourself questions such as: Is it something I can begin part-time? Am I physically able to do it? Are there any special licenses or permits I will need? What kind of equipment am I going to need? Will I need a special vehicle? Tools? Am I going to need a computer, printer, catalogs or brochures? Will I use my home phone, my cell phone or a new number?

Refer to the following list to assist you in calculating what you will need to start your new venture and what it will cost you up front.

Estimated Start-Up Costs

Expense	Cost
Advertising	
Bank Charges	
Cell Phone	
Credit Cards	
Dues	
Estimated Quarterly Taxes	
Fuel	
Gifts Given	
Legal Fees	
Licenses	
Permits	
Liability Insurance	
Vehicle Insurance	
Vehicle Payment	
Vehicle Maintenance	
Office Supply	
Office Equipment	
Office Furniture	
Office Rent	
Postage	

Printing	
Service Supplies	
Fax Line	
Internet Service	
Work Clothing	
Utilities	
Subscriptions	
Payroll	
Payroll taxes	
Workmen's Comp Ins	
Toll Fees	
Other	
Total Estimated Beginning Fees	

Total up the initial costs and determine if that fits your beginning budget. If it does, then you are well on your way to entrepreneurship. Chances are, you already have an idea of what you want to do.

If, on the other hand, the start-up costs are larger than you can afford, what items can you do without at the beginning? Are any of the items you need already around your home or is someone you know willing to loan these items to you temporarily? Are the items you need available on "Craig's List," swap meets, garage sales or in your friend's garage or storage unit? My daughter completely furnished her two-bedroom apartment for her and her two children for less than $300.00. People were either selling their items on-line or just giving things away. I was amazed!

If you are short on cash, and most businesses are in the beginning, bootstrap yourself into your new business. Tell everyone you know about your new venture. Enlist their help in securing the items you need. You will be surprised how fast and from which direction these items will appear. Really!

My first desk in a spare bedroom was a Masonite door and two wooden sawhorses for legs. It all cost me about $20.00 in 1978. I added a touch-tone telephone and an electric typewriter and *voila!* My office was ready to go! Thereafter, as your new venture produces cash flow, you can add the equipment you need until you are well on your way.

However, you may find that what you thought you were going to do originally is not as interesting or as viable as you thought. Do you know someone already in the business that would be willing to help you get started? A mentor can be a great asset in getting your new venture up and going. Finding someone who has already trod the path you are pursuing can often mean the difference between success and disappointment. Most successful people are happy to share their knowledge with someone who is 'serious' about their chosen field. In fact, many successful business owners see their position as a 'calling' in life.

Why do I emphasize doing your 'homework' first? Because I speak Japanese, I had the opportunity years ago to work with several Japanese businessmen putting together a joint venture in the United States. When I met with them to discuss how we were going to begin, they asked numerous questions. A lot of questions! In fact, they asked questions down to the smallest detail possible. After several long days of constant questions and information gathering, I eventually became irritated and finally asked why so many questions? They replied that there were many other departments that had to sign off on this venture and they wanted to have answers to everyone's questions back in Tokyo. I was still irritated because I thought we could just print some brochures, import the products and I would do the selling. What I learned from this experience was that by doing the homework in detail up front, the implementation and the speed of how things grew thereafter was nothing short of amazing.

The old adage, "Find a need and fill it" is still true today. Keep your eyes open for an opportunity to fill a need that people want, but is not being filled or addressed properly. Can you take a current business or concept and add value to it? That's what Starbucks did with coffee. They took an otherwise boring commodity that everyone purchased and raised it to a new level. Do not skip over this area of investigation. This preparation stage is so important. If you do your homework properly, the implementation will be much easier and faster.

WARNING! Do your homework in the beginning and you will have fewer headaches during the implementation phase of your business. The important thing is to get up and going as soon as possible. We can all get more *'things'* and more money. What we can't get back is *'more time.'* One of my favorite sayings that I learned from my wife is *"Begin… the rest is easy."*

The term for 'doing your homework' in the business world is known as *'performing your due diligence.'* If, after you do your 'due diligence,' the answer is 'No' to your chosen idea, go back to your original list and look at another Category 1 idea. Then, go down the list and ask yourself those same questions as before. "Will I start full-time or part-time? Should I begin in my house or in an office?"

When you have weighed all the pros and cons and you have decided upon your new venture, it's time for one more exercise. Turn to the next chapter to find out.

Marshall's Rule # 3

The '7 P's of Preparation'

Prior Proper Preparation Prevents Poor Pathetic Performance

CHAPTER 8

Step 2:
A Name To Remember

"What's in a name? Everything!

Now that you have decided what type of business to begin and what your monthly expenses will be, now comes the fun part. Naming your new venture. Giving your new company a name can be one of the most important things you will do to position your business in the minds of people. Calling yourself XYZ Enterprises tells your potential customers almost nothing about what you do. On the other hand, **Mike's Discount Plumbing Service** creates a vivid picture in the mind of your prospects. Keeping things simple can make it easier for your prospects to identify whom you are and what you do. Before that happens, **you**, of course, must identify who you are and what you do.

Here's a simple exercise. In 10 words or less, describe what it is you do. *"I fix plumbing leaks and clean drains"* is simple and straightforward. This is called the 'elevator presentation.' You should be able to tell people what it is you do in the time it takes an elevator to reach the next floor. Go ahead now and fill in the blanks below:

The name of my company is:

____

____

When people ask me what it is that I do, I say:

____

____

____

Remember to keep it simple, descriptive and possibly fun. I have a friend who started a website marketing company called 'Lemonade Stand.' The image of a young entrepreneur standing on a street corner selling cold lemonade on a hot day brings back memories of simplicity when things were fun. Be sure and have fun with this exercise.

Once you have decided upon a name, you will need to file what is called a 'Fictitious Business Name Statement' if you decide to be a sole proprietor. This is usually accomplished by going to your local county recorder or the county clerk's office. Once there, you will need to do a 'name search' to determine if someone else already has the name you want. This is performed by looking up the name(s) in a computer or on-line at home. You can do this yourself for free or pay a nominal fee to have the recorder/clerk do this for you. You may be able to complete the application and name search on-line if your jurisdiction offers this service. Because someone else may have already 'taken' the name you want, it's a good idea to be prepared with a few backup names for your new business, just in case. You can learn more about how to do this in the next chapter under 'Finalizing Your Entity Name.'

If you are going to begin with a corporation, you may need to file with your local Secretary of State's office or other governmental agency in your jurisdiction. Be prepared for high fees. A good CPA should be able to assist you in this endeavor. Another option if you choose to 'incorporate' is *Legalzoom.com*.[1]

That's all there is here. We're keeping it short and simple. Now that you have a unique or descriptive name for your new venture, let's look at what type of business structure would be best for you and your new venture.

[1] We do not endorse nor have any affiliation with www.Legalzoom.com

CHAPTER 9

Step 3: Choosing Your Business Structure

Formal education will make you a living:
Self-education will make you a fortune.
—Jim Rohn

Once you have chosen the field and a name that can bring you fame and fortune, you will next need to decide what type of business structure you will use to pursue your dreams.

WARNING: This is a very important step. There are several different types of business structures to choose from. I have listed the most common types of business structures with examples of their pros and cons. As laws vary by state, you may want to consult a Certified Public Accountant or other tax professional as to which business structure will work best for you in regards to taxation. You may also want to consult with an attorney to protect any assets you may currently own. Gather information from reputable sources and then decide which of these courses of action will work best for you.

Sole Proprietor

The most common legal structure is that of a sole proprietorship. It's the least costly way to begin a new business venture. The sole proprietor personally owns and operates the business. All income derived from the sole proprietorship passes through to the business owner. Likewise, all taxes, debts and liabilities pass through to the business owner as part of their personal liability.

As of this writing, many of your medical insurance premiums can be tax deductible. You can also hire your spouse, deduct their income as an expense and enjoy the income. Of course, the spouse must pay taxes on their income.

The sole proprietor receives all the income. All your business related expenses are also tax deductible. These tax deductions are a major benefit of being self-employed. This is the upside.

The downside? As a sole-proprietor, you also inherit all the risk. If you are slapped with a lawsuit, your home and other personal assets are also at risk. All liabilities are your responsibility. All profits, tax-deductions and liability pass through to the sole proprietor personally. Once, while I was working at a project, my parked truck somehow rolled down a hill and very expertly knocked down a block wall at the end of the street. My vehicle insurance paid for the damage. If the damage had exceeded my policy limits, my personal assets could have been at risk.

As you begin your business, be sure to walk around with a big "L" on your forehead. (No, not 'Loser'.) It stands for 'Liability'. A good **commercial liability insurance** policy is something you will definitely want to own as a business owner, regardless of which business structure you choose.

In everything you do, do it properly and think before you talk or act. As I said, a sole-proprietor is the easiest way to start a business. However, later as you hire employees, you will want to consider another type of business entity. Remember, your goal is to build a business that will run itself without you being there. This involves hiring and training employees how to properly operate your business. You also want to protect yourself and your hard earned assets.

Advantages of a Sole Proprietorship

- A sole proprietor has complete control and decision-making power over the business.
- The sale or transfer of the business can take place at the discretion of the sole proprietor.
- Minimal legal costs or documentation to forming a sole proprietorship.
- Few formal business requirements or corporate meetings.
- Profits from the business flow-through directly to the owner's personal tax return, with IRS form 'Schedule C' attached for business deductions. (Woo-whoo!)

Disadvantages of a Sole Proprietorship

- The sole proprietor can be held personally liable for the debts and obligations of the business.
- The sole proprietor is at risk for any liabilities incurred as a result of acts committed by employees.
- The sole proprietor's business and personal assets are at combined risk.
- The sole proprietor must file and pay quarterly tax payments.

Even with all the liability in your court, sole proprietorships are still the most common form of business organization by a wide margin. As recently reported, there were approximately over 22,000,000 sole proprietorships, 3,000,000 partnerships and almost 6,000,000 corporations in the United States. [1]

Partnership

A partnership is when two or more individuals come together and agree to begin a business between them. I suggest that some key decisions need to be made BEFORE a partnership is concluded.

Who is in charge of day-to-day operations? Who is authorized to sign contracts with customers or suppliers on the partnership's behalf? Are there to be any silent partners? Silent or limited partners are those who put in capital to the venture, but have no say in the daily workings of the business. Who will be the treasurer?

A partnership itself is not really a taxable entity. A partnership files an informational tax return known as Form 1065 and is attached to each partner's personal tax return.

It lists the partnership's income and expenses, and the amount of profits or loss accruing to each partner. All income received by either partner is passed through and taxed similar to a sole proprietorship. All liabilities are pro-rated. This means that you are liable only to the extent of how much money or other assets you contributed to the business partnership.

Because of these issues, I highly recommend you find a competent attorney to write the contract or agreement between you and your partner(s). Because of my own personal experience within a partnership, I don't recommend it as a viable possibility. Yes, two heads are often better than one, but any obligation your partner(s) enters into or mistakes made also obligates you as well. So be careful. Good friends in business can soon become not so good friends and may not be a good mix.

Advantages of a Partnership

- An added source of capital to start the business.
- Someone else with specialized knowledge or experience.
- An additional head to discuss business ideas with.
- Someone who can operate the business if you become ill or incapacitated.

Disadvantages of a Partnership

- Bad behavior of a partner can cause negative consequences for you.
- If your partner dies, their spouse or companion may become your new partner.

C Corporation

The most common type of corporation is a C Corporation. This is a for-profit, state-incorporated business. Articles of Incorporation must be filed and appropriate fees are to be paid to set it up with the state.

The C Corporation is a very interesting business entity. It takes on a separate tax and liability identity from that of the owner(s). Inside a C Corporation, you pay yourself a salary. The salary is treated as a tax deduction within the corporation and you pay the normal tax rates on your personal (employee) tax return. This allows the business owner(s) to be removed from personal liability for debts incurred by the corporation. If your business goes bankrupt or is hit with a lawsuit, the owner(s) personal assets are protected. Only the business assets are at risk. This is one of the biggest reasons many businesses choose to incorporate. Also, as a separate entity, a corporation can own property, make business deals or even sue another business. All of this can be performed independently of the owner(s).

Advantages of a C Corporation

- The corporation is a separate legal entity from the owner(s).
- Corporations can deduct corporate benefit health plan costs as an operating expense.
- If a stockholder dies or wants to sell their shares, the corporation may still continue.

- The owner(s) personal assets are protected against lawsuits or judgments.

Disadvantages of a C Corporation

- *Double taxation can occur if there are any* dividends to the owner(s) and are taxed again at the applicable tax rate.
- State regulations must be followed very closely. Failure to do so can cause fines or other legal hassles.
- It costs more to start a C Corp than a sole proprietorship or partnership.
- Annual stockholder meetings must be held.
- There are additional governmental regulations and hoops to jump through.
- Annual fees may be required to be paid to the state.

S Corporation

An S Corporation is formed similarly as a C Corporation. Once the business has incorporated, the owner(s) can decide to file as an S Corporation, usually within 75-90 days of incorporating. You will need to file an IRS Form 2553. This will not create a different type of corporation, but it will change the way the corporation is taxed. The owner(s) or partner(s) of an S Corporation are taxed similar to a sole proprietorship or a partnership. Income (or losses) are *'passed through'* to the owner(s) on a pro rata basis in proportion to their invested capital and is reported on their individual tax return. This is my favored form for a business.

Advantages of an S Corporation

- Corporate losses can be passed through and you may be able to deduct the losses from your personal tax return.
- Liability is to the corporation only.

- Expenses and or deductions can be passed through to the owner(s).

Disadvantages of an S Corporation

- Additional paperwork and rules to keep up with compared to a sole proprietor.
- Just as a C Corporation, it may be costly to set up and continue.
- You must be a U.S. citizen to utilize the S Corporation entity.
- An S corporation's earnings are taxed, whether they are retained by the corporation or paid to the shareholders

Limited Liability Corporation (LLC)

An LLC, although a business entity, is a type of unincorporated association and is not a corporation. It is more of a hybrid of a corporation and a sole proprietorship. The primary characteristic an LLC shares with a corporation is the limited liability aspect and the primary characteristic it shares with a sole proprietorship is the availability of pass-through income and tax deductions. It is often more flexible than a corporation and it is well-suited for companies with a single owner. LLCs are popular because, similar to a corporation, owners have limited personal liability for the debts and actions of the LLC. Other features of LLCs are more like a partnership or sole proprietorship, providing management flexibility and the benefit of pass-through taxation.

The federal government does not currently recognize an LLC as a classification for federal tax purposes. Therefore, an LLC business entity must file either a corporation, partnership or sole proprietorship tax return. An LLC can also elect to be taxed as an S Corporation. With an LLC, you will file both a corporation and a personal income tax return.

Finalizing Your Entity Name

Now that we have waded through the boring, legal mumbo jumbo, let's get this business party started, shall we? You've now decided what to name your new company and you've done your research and decided which business structure to operate under. Now it's time to make your new venture a legal enterprise.

Since the sole proprietorship is the easiest and least expensive business structure to begin, we will use this format in our example.

You will need to file a **'Fictitious Business Name Statement.'** Either filling out a form online or going to your local county recorder or the county clerk's office usually accomplishes this. Once there, you will need to do a 'name search' to determine if someone else already has the name you want. This is performed by looking up the name(s) in a computer or on a microfiche slide. You can do this yourself for free or pay a nominal fee to have the recorder/clerk do this for you. Because someone else may have already 'chosen' the name you want, it's a good idea to prepared with a few backup names for your new business, just in case.

If the business name you desire is not listed, then hooray! Go ahead and claim the name. You do this by filling out the 'Fictitious Business Name Statement' form to begin the process of establishing your company name. This usually means providing your name, address, telephone number and what business structure you will use. (Sole proprietor, corporation, LLC) They may also ask what the name of the new venture will be, the names of company officers, when the business has or will start and an emergency contact number. Be sure to complete all the necessary information. Once this has been accomplished, take the completed form and your checkbook to the recorder/clerk window. Filing fees vary by jurisdiction, but are normally under $100.00.

Publishing your legal name

Next, you will need to publish your new company name in a newspaper. Often times, the county recorder/clerk will provide you with a list of approved newspapers in your area in which to publish your new name. **Warning:** Large daily newspapers will often overcharge you for this service. I recommend choosing a small, independent legal newspaper that specializes in filing new business statements. This normally costs under $75.00.

You will normally have 30 days to publish your new name. This is your responsibility. The county recorder/clerk will not do this for you. In a week or so, the publishing newspaper will send you a copy of the legal notice that was published. Keep this copy in your permanent business records, as you may need this from time to time. Also, when you go to the bank to set up a new business checking account, the bank may ask to see a copy of your business statement and proof that you have published your legal name in an approved newspaper.

In today's litigious society, it is good practice to protect you and your assets. Just like the story of the Three Pigs, if you are working by yourself and operate as a sole proprietor, you have a house made of straw or sticks. If you operate as a corporation or an LLC, you have built a house made of bricks. Eventually, you will want to place your business and other assets in a trust. This is similar to placing a wall around your property to keep the big bad wolf (lawsuits, Uncle Sam) from taking what is yours. Once you have done this, it's now time to order business cards, stationery and other business forms. Woo-whoo!

A great place to get additional information is by going to: http://www.360financialliteracy.org/Topics/Owning-a-Business/Starting-a-Business

[1] From the Statistical Abstract of the United States: 2015

CHAPTER 10

Step 4:
Looking For A Rich Uncle

"You can complain about a lack of money, or you can do something about it."

■ *Martin Hurlburt*

Now that you've decided which business to start, what you are going to name it and which business structure you will use, we next decide how we are going to finance your new venture. There are several ways you can do this. The easiest and most obvious way to start a business is from cash already on hand. If you have enough savings set aside, congratulations. If you don't have a pile of dusty money sitting around like most of us, there are other ways to get your new venture up and running. Following are a few suggested ways to come up with your starting capital.

401(k)

First, let's start with some cash you may already have and not realized you could use it. Do you have a 401(k) or IRA? Depending upon your plan rules, you may be able to swing a loan from your 401(k) or Individual Retirement Account (IRA). Check with your account administrator about the requirements of drawing a loan from your qualified plan. We're talking about a 'loan', not a withdrawal. Once your business is up and running and producing a cash flow, pay back the loan as soon as possible. This is part of your retirement. If you are already retired, you may have already rolled over your 401(k) to and IRA or annuity. Find out if there are any surrender charges or rules to 'borrowing' from these accounts.

Cash Value Life Insurance

Do you have a life insurance policy with a cash value account attached to it? This could be a Universal Life Policy, an Equity Index Policy, a Whole Life Policy or a Variable Universal Life Policy. Consider a policy *'loan'* from this account. In many cases, a 'loan' is tax-free and may never be necessary to be paid back in your lifetime. However, it is always advisable to pay back the loan as soon as possible. If you 'withdraw' funds from your policy, you may be required to pay taxes on any interest you may have earned. Check with your insurance agent or advisor for the plan of action that best fits your situation. Many plans charge 3%–5% percent interest per year for a policy loan. That's a lot better than what a bank loan will cost you. It may make sense to 'borrow' *your* money to produce a cash-flow enterprise. If you don't have one of these policies, does a relative or friend have one of these policies that would like to generate a larger return on their investment? Then, you can pay them an agreed amount of interest until you pay back the loan. If you have a straight 'Term' insurance policy, there usually is not a separate cash account attached to this type of policy.

Home Equity Loan

Accessing equity in your home may be an alternative. As always, use caution when contemplating this option. A home equity loan adds additional money to the principal of your home loan and will need to be paid back. Always seek professional advice from a reputable source.

Venture Capital

We've all seen the television program where business owners seeking money for their venture explain their new idea to a group of wealthy individuals who are sitting on the stage. Some of their ideas are crazy and some of their plans evoke a bidding war among the wealthy venture capitalists. Borrowing from a venture capitalist may be a viable way of getting your new venture off the ground.

The positive side of this equation is an infusion of cash and usually a wealth of experience from your new partner(s). The possible negative of this scenario is that yes, you now have others who hold a major stake in your new business. You may have to give up some control of your company while you use their money. And yes, be ready to explain, in minute detail, how you are going to use their money and how and when you are going to pay them back. Tread carefully here!

Angels

Do you have a rich uncle or someone with cash that believes in your idea? Is there someone in your circle of contacts or acquaintances that would like to invest in a business venture while earning interest on that investment? These people are called 'Angels' because they usually come with less risk and drama than venture capitalists (or your mom!)

Sell Assets

The *best way* to start a new business is with your own money. Do you have large ticket items around your home that you could sell? Do you have items such as an extra vehicle, motorcycle, boat, RV or quad runner? Instead of making payments on these items, turn them into cash by selling them and using the cash for your new venture.

Do you look at your 'toys' and think you are just not able to part with these items? Is there a way you could 'rent' these toys out and make a profit? Then, use the profits to make the monthly payment on the 'toy' and use the remaining cash to finance your new business. Be sure to buy liability insurance if you rent out these items. Another option is to 'pawn' your items for cash and then buy them back later.

Micro Loans

A 'Micro Loan' is where you borrow a small amount of money from an individual. These loans are typically in the $25.00 to $200.00 range. Maybe this is all you need to get up and running. I started my first business venture with $700.00. I borrowed $500.00 from my brother and the remaining $200.00 came from my own pocket. Start small and generate a cash flow of your own. Then, build momentum and keep going and never look back. Oh, the sweet smell of success!

Seller Financing

Maybe you've decided to purchase an existing business. Will the seller *'carry the paper'* for you? This means the owner will sell the business to you on 'terms' negotiated by both you the buyer and the seller. You operate the business while paying the owner a set amount of money on a predetermined schedule according to the 'terms' you both agreed upon. This relieves you of having to come up with a large down payment and maybe the owner will stay on as a consultant to help manage *(keep an eye on)* the business.

Or, maybe the owner wants to take some time off while you manage the business on a trial basis. This is where the two of you can be very creative. Find out what the seller's hot button is, (their reason for selling), and solve that issue for them. **Warning:** *Be sure to put everything in writing!*

Government Loans

The 'Small Business Administration' (SBA) is a government-sponsored program to assist small and medium sized businesses. Loan programs can include those for women, minorities or veterans. The Small Business Administration (SBA) 7(a) Loan Guarantee program is probably the most popular loan offered by the agency. It is their basic SBA loan program. SBA 7(a) loans are for a maximum up to $2 million. The terms of SBA 7(a) loans are 25 years for real estate and/or equipment and up to 7 years for start-up or working capital. Interest rates are based on the prime rate, the size of the loan and the length of time for the loan. SBA 7(a) loans can be used for purchasing land or buildings, equipment, machinery or supplies; long or short-term working capital; for refinancing; or for the purchase of an already existing business.

If the borrower has funds available from other sources, an SBA loan may not be granted. This type of loan is funded through SBA approved banks in your local area. Check your local SBA office for a list of approved banks in your area. This may be a good way to finance your new start-up, but be prepared for a mountain of paperwork and a lot of time.

Borrowing From Family or A Friend

If you have a family member or a good friend, you might ask that person to 'co-sign' a loan for you. As a co-signer, they don't have to give up their own money. They are guaranteeing their personal name and/or credit that the loan will be paid back in the event you don't make the monthly payments. Put everything in writing, including all the terms of payback, the interest rate, and what happens if you default on the loan. Don't accept just a handshake; put it in writing. This will prevent any 'confusion' in the future.

Paying back the loan and including interest is a great good-faith gesture, and it may save the relationship. Here's a suggestion to keep your friend a friend; use an outside loan servicing agency to write the loan agreement, collect the money and pay the lender (your friend or family member.) An example would be ZimpleMoney. Com.[1]

Partner Financing

Maybe you have a friend or family member who believes in what you are going to do. Ask them to be a *silent partner*. A silent partner is an individual who provides funding to the business as their only contribution. A silent partner, sometimes called a limited partner, will also experience less exposure to liability because they do not participate in the daily operations of the business. This means they have 'ownership' in the new business, but no say in the day-to-day operations. When there is a profit, you may share this with them or agree in other ways to compensate them for their investment in the business.

These are all options to consider. See? Now you're getting creative. This way, you retain ownership of your assets. As mentioned before, the best way to start a new business is with your own money. No one is looking over your shoulder telling you how to run your business.

Establishing Business Credit

As soon as you start your business, you should work on establishing a business credit record. Here are my suggestions for building your business credit: Get a business credit card and use it 'wisely' for your beginning business purchases. Pay off the balance each month as soon as you can.

Set up a credit account with vendors and suppliers for equipment, materials and office supplies. Pay off these accounts promptly.

Get a bank account and operate your business as a "real" business, paying bills through this account rather than your personal account. It shows you are *'for real'* and gives you credibility when you want to get a loan later.

Most new businesses use personal credit while they are starting out. However, using your personal credit for business can be risky. Using personal credit for business can put your own personal credit in jeopardy. If you fail to pay back your business bills, your personal credit rating can be affected.

[1] No solicitation for insurance or securities is offered here nor do we endorse www. *ZimpleMoney.com or any other similar type of enterprise.*

CHAPTER 11

Step 5: Creating Your Image

"Use a picture. It's worth a thousand words."

- Arthur Brisbane to the Syracuse Advertising Men's Club, March 1911

How you position your new business venture can be the difference between starting quickly and no one noticing you at all. I started a pest control business years ago called *Marshall Exterminating*. Most people understood what it was I was doing by the name. Yet, I took it a step further. When I began, I wore dark trousers, a white knit polo shirt with my company name embroidered on the shirt, a dark blue navy cap and a cell phone with an antenna.

I was once out soliciting apartment complexes to offer my services. As I was nearing the front entrance to the apartment manager's office, a young man who was sitting in the office saw me coming and only saw the word *'Marshall'* on my shirt. With the dark cap and the cell phone with 'antenna', he apparently felt guilty about something and assumed I was there to arrest him. He quickly fled out the back door of the office. As I entered the office, the apartment manager noticed who I really was and began laughing profusely. He called the young man back inside explaining that I was indeed not the police. And yes, I acquired a new client.

Again, how you position yourself in the minds of your potential customers is very important. I suggest you create a *'Hook.'* What do I mean by a 'Hook?' A local carpet cleaning business in my area is called *"Pinks Carpet Cleaning and Restoration."* Their 'Hook' is *"If it's dirty and stinks, call Pinks."* Their vans and business cards are all pink! My *Marshall Exterminating* representatives handed out magnets with my name and telephone number in the shape of a sheriff's 5-pointed badge. Think of a *'Hook'* that you can use to create an image your clients will remember you by. The old adage, *"Use a picture. It's worth a thousand words"* is still true today. Create a picture of what you do in the minds of people so they can understand what it is you do and will want to do business with you.

Sometimes, a company vehicle, brochure or business card will list way too much information. This can often confuse a potential client. Don't attempt to relate everything you know or do in your communication with people. Remember to be informative, yet to the point. Create interest in the minds of your potential clients so they will pick up the phone and call about your product or service and ask questions.

You will always want to keep a positive business image in the minds of your prospects. There needs to be a balance between a positive business image and over spending. If you need invoices (and most of us do) you can begin with invoice templates available from most office product software programs. These templates can be found on Quicken, Microsoft Works or Microsoft Money.

Many stationery or office supply stores sell ready-made invoice or sales slip booklets. I started with a form I typed out on my typewriter. I made multiple copies, placed a carbon copy paper between my two forms and put them on a clipboard. I was ready to go for just pennies. (Both the typewriter and carbon copy sheets show my age!)

If you think you can create a form yourself and want a professional looking paper to print it on, check with a local paper supply company. They carry many types of colored and pre-printed design papers you can put through a computer printer. If you have a few extra dollars and want to get extra fancy, go to www.paperdirect.com. They offer a large variety of paper frames, invitations, business cards, brochure blanks, etc. If you visit www.nebs.com you will find almost anything you need for business printing. My favorite for invoices and keeping track of who owes me money is MyInvoices & Estimates® Deluxe 10. Go to Avanquest.com and choose the 'Business' tab. You can set-up multiple businesses with this one program. Or, use a professional printing company from your mastermind group.

Marshall's Rule # 4

"Look and act like a professional business person and people will assume you are."

Once again, we do not endorse or receive remuneration for www.paperdirect.com, www.nebs.com or MyInvoices & Estimates. Use your best judgement.

CHAPTER 12

Step 6: Promoting Your New Venture

The greatest security is to plan and act, and take the risk that will ultimately ensure your personal freedom and independence."

– Dennis Waitley

Now it's time to prepare and structure one of the most important aspects of your new venture. Getting the word out to prospective clients or customers is a never-ending activity. There is what I call 'The Three Foot Rule.' Talk to everyone you know within three feet of you. With a big smile on your face, hand out your business card and let people know what it is that you do. However, do not walk down the street handing these out to people willy-nilly. That's a waste of business cards and your time. You are looking for people who are looking for you. Right? You need to position yourself where people will see you.

Always remember that the first item you sell is yourself. People buy YOU! There are several ways you can advertise your new venture. This is called 'Marketing 101.'

Examples include:

Word of Mouth	Social Media
Networking	Advertising
Referrals	Business Cards
Yellow Pages	Door Hangers
Website Marketing	Magnets, pens, etc.
	Yelp.com

Promoting yourself and your company should become second nature to you. As mentioned earlier, your elevator presentation should be brief, yet create a picture in the mind of your prospect of exactly what it is that you do. It's the A-B-C of Marketing 101: **A**lways **B**e **C**ontacting.

Word of Mouth Reviews

This is by far the best way to promote your business. Having someone talk positively about you and how you helped him or her is a great way to build a business. We all want to be treated fairly when we need a repair or help with a particular situation.

My mother always told me to do a good job for other people. She said, "Do the job so well, you would sign your name to it." When doing work for other people, wow them with your excellent work. Then, follow up with a 'thank you' card. Maybe call them in a few days and ask if everything was to their satisfaction. Most people appreciate this. Keep in contact with them periodically. They may need your services again in the future. Be sure to keep a list of people you have performed work for. Periodically send them a promotional ad or email about a special you may be offering.

Networking

Networking is a must in today's business world. Everyone is bombarded daily with too much information. Networking with other like-minded individuals and business owners who will refer you puts a positive light on your business and separates you from all the others. Cultivate relationships with those that I call 'gatekeepers.' These are people who know other people who may want to do business with you and can give you an introduction.

Let me give you an example. I call it 'The Wedding Mafia.' Jane and Richard are going to get married in three months. Jane goes shopping for a wedding dress. She shops around and finally finds the 'right' gown. In her conversation with the wedding dress shop owner, she mentions that she is going to look wonderful in her wedding pictures. Mary, the wedding dress shop owner, suggests she call a business associate of hers who does wedding photography.

Jane takes the card of the wedding photographer and makes an appointment to meet him. At the meeting, Jerry, the photographer, asks Jane what kind of wedding cake she is thinking about having at her wedding reception. Jane hasn't decided yet or even knows whom to call. Jerry gives Jane the card of a fellow business associate who operates a bakery there in the neighborhood and gives Bob, the baker, a glowing review. Jerry also offers the business card of an associate, Lance, who is a DJ for weddings and parties.

Lance, in his conversation with Jane and Richard, asks what kind of flowers they are thinking about for the wedding. Lance gives them the name of Cheryl, a local florist.

Jane is thrilled. She didn't have to go through the internet or drive all over town interviewing and choosing the people she will need for her wedding. She already has too many other things to arrange for her big day.

Unknown to Jane and Richard, Mary, the dress storeowner, is friends with Jerry the photographer, Bob the baker, and Lance the DJ and

Cheryl the florist. They all work together to promote each other's business. This is a perfect example of the adage *'givers gain.'*

Your job is to establish relationships with other 'gatekeepers' that compliment your business and you can refer to each other for business. This is also referred to as a 'Mastermind Group.'

Referrals

Referrals are the best kind of business leads you will ever receive. Treat these referrals and the person who passed them to you with respect. In most cases, the prospective client has already heard about you from the person giving you the referral. They have told the prospective client how good you are and you should do the same when referring others. Always be sure to send a 'thank you' to the person who referred you. This helps to build the relationship with your 'gatekeepers.'

Yellow Pages

Many years ago, you were not a legitimate business unless you had a listing or a display ad in the local yellow pages. Today, technology has advanced. I have found that it is now easier to look up the 'yellow pages' on the Internet. That old phone book that is delivered to your driveway or doorstep is now either thrown away or used as a doorstop.

It's much easier and faster to look something up on the Internet. Google Ads or Yelp.com are a great way to advertise and receive referrals for your business. I have found that having a listing on the Internet as well as a simple web page can drive people to you and compliment your networking efforts. With a web page and the Internet, you have the option of changing how your potential clients see your business 24/7.

Website Marketing

I'm a baby-boomer. I came to the Website marketing party late. I wasn't sure if I really needed a Website or even how to do it myself. Hey! I'm an entrepreneur. No one can do it as well as I can! Right? Wrong! There are a myriad of Website services available. Ask around and ask for a 'referral.' Many Website promoters provide a 'cafeteria menu' plan to choose which services you want to set up at a very reasonable cost. Here again, look for someone who has expertise in the social media field. If you are short of funds, and most start-ups are, start small and work your way up to where you want to be in regards to your social media campaigns.

Print Advertising

Advertising comes in all forms. You can 'wrap' your car or truck with graphics, print brochures, business cards, post cards and other items to hand out. You can also do billboard, radio and television advertising. The list and methods are almost endless.

A Final Word

Throughout this book, I have used the term 'client' rather than customer. Webster's Dictionary defines a 'customer' as *"someone you sell something to."* The word 'client' is defined as *"someone who is placed under your protection."* The key to building great business relationships is to treat ALL of those with whom you do business as a 'client,' taking them *"under your protection"* rather than *"someone you sell something to."* People will usually notice you going the extra mile and are more likely to refer you to their friends and neighbors. It's all about trust. Isn't it? Don't worry. Often, business starts slow, but be patient.

If you follow these steps as outlined in this book, one day soon, you will wake up and be hard pressed to get all of your work accomplished in one day. That's the day you can look forward to enjoying!

Want an 'instant' mastermind group? Check out BNI.com. It stands for Business Networking International. It's the largest business referral networking organization in the world. A great way to keep business relationships alive is by using a service called *'SendOutCards.com.'* You can automatically send a thank you card or almost any type of card to your past or prospective clients. They will print and mail the card for you. It's a great service to keep in contact with people as well as a way to promote your business.

CHAPTER 13

Step 7: The Power of Multiples

"I would rather have 1% of the efforts of 100 people than 100% of my own efforts."

■ *J. Paul Getty – Oil Industrialist*

One of the most important lessons I learned from being in business for myself is that you cannot do it all yourself. If you try to do it all yourself, at some point down the road, you will experience that wonderful result of constant hard work. It's called ***'burnout.'*** Yes. In the beginning, it may all be up to you. But sometime in your career as a businessperson, you need to train someone else to do the daily work you are doing. A common misbelief among entrepreneurs is that *"nobody can do it as good as I can"* or *"it's just easier to do it myself than take the time to train someone else."*

I learned the following lesson several years after I had started my first business. I worked hard each day and came home exhausted. I soon realized that my income was not going to increase much past a certain point because there was only so much I could do by myself. This answer was given to me when I was talking to a client of mine who owned a Baskin-Robbins ice cream store. It would be years later before I came to understand what he was saying. He said, *"I realized the other day that I can only serve up so many scoops of ice cream a day by myself."* There really is a limit to how much you can do by yourself. While I was in high school, I worked in a fast food restaurant. I started out at the drink machine and then graduated to the fryer and then to the grill as I learned how to do everything. Finally, I found myself taking orders at the window and adding up the totals in my head. (This was long before 'smart' cash registers.)

If I had tried to do all of these tasks by myself at the restaurant, most of the customers would have gone away mad and not returned because of the slow service. (It so happened that my brother, two cousins and best friend ended up working with me. Boy! The stories I could tell.)

The illustration below gives you a picture of what I mean.

You - The Power of One

All by yourself

The Team -
The Power of Delegation

"Let" others do it for you while you have a life.

The most important thing you can do for your business is to train others to do the work you were doing and then get out of the way. This allows you to step back and lead, manage and orchestrate what is going on. You teach others how to be a clone of yourself so you can leave and *'have a life'* instead of being tied down to your 'job.' In other words, work 'on' your business, not 'in' your business. If you continue to stay a one-person show, all you have done for yourself is to have 'bought' your own J-O-B. As I mentioned before, that stands for "Just Over Broke." Is this why you want to go into business for yourself? Of course not! By teaching others and collapsing time frames, you can become financially independent faster than trying to do it all yourself. Believe me, I have tried to do it eight times. It doesn't work. Period! End of discussion!

Eventually, your new business needs to run and operate without you physically having to be there. Remember, you are building the Golden Goose!

CHAPTER 14

Step 8: Putting the Pieces Together

"Never tell a man he cannot do something, while he is doing it."

- Old Chinese Proverb

The time has now arrived to put your plan into action. It's time to strike out on your own and be the person you were born to be. Are you scared? It's natural to be afraid or unsure in the beginning. Don't worry. It's going to be fun. Soon, you will look back and ask yourself, *"Why didn't I do this sooner?"*

You came up with an idea. You've completed your due diligence (homework) and decided what type of business to create. You completed your paperwork and now have a legal name. You know fairly well what equipment and/or supplies you are going to need at the beginning and how much it is going to cost. Your invoices, brochures and business cards have been printed. Exciting isn't it?

Now it's time to begin talking to everyone around you and letting him or her know that you are open for business. If things start out slow, don't worry. Just keep going forward. You've made a decision to press forward. Have faith in yourself and your idea and follow through with your new venture. Many people try for a few weeks or months and when not much happens, they throw up their hands and say, *"See. I didn't think it would work."* It's the old adage, *"If you think you can, you can. If you think you can't, you can't."* Remember, have faith in yourself.

As time goes by, your business will pick up speed until finally you are on autopilot. Don't give up. See yourself in your mind being successful. Looks and feels good, doesn't it?

As you begin your new venture, you are going to make a lot of mistakes. That is a fact of life. You are going to learn what works and what doesn't. Congratulations! This is all part of the game. It's called experience. Experience is one of the greatest teachers of wisdom in the world, is it not? There is only so much I can teach you in this book. Some things you will need to experience for yourself. However, if you follow the steps I have outlined here, you will not make any fatal mistakes that will throw all of your hard work down the drain. Babe Ruth, the great baseball player said, *"Every strike brings me closer to the next home run."* As you progress through your learning curve, you will make fewer and fewer mistakes until you rarely make any mistakes. That is the day to look forward to.

In our world today, people have been trained to study, graduate and get a job and make someone else wealthy. Because of this climate, there is a significant amount of negative misinformation about starting a business. When many people start a business of their own, they are often mocked and laughed at by those who have been programmed to never even try. So what! I bet that most of them fought to get into the company of their choice and are probably now fighting to get out. Let them laugh at you while you *laugh out loud all the way to the bank!* Persevere. Press forward in your goal of building a golden goose. It will all be worth it!

What sets apart an entrepreneur from an employee? Employees trade their *time* for money. Entrepreneurs trade their *ideas* for money. Employees are *problem* oriented while entrepreneurs are *solution* oriented. Most employees have *pipedreams* where entrepreneurs have a *vision*. Where employees *compete*, entrepreneurs *create*. Employees try to *avoid* risk whereas entrepreneurs learn to *manage* risk. Employees seek for *security* and entrepreneurs seek for *freedom*. Finally, employees want to be *comfortable* while entrepreneurs are comfortable being uncomfortable because they are in *control of their lives.*[1]

Now it is time to *'put the pieces together'*. This is where the rubber meets the road. This is where your 'homework' comes together. I have included a 'Business Start-Up Checklist' at the end of this chapter. Start at the top of the list and work your way down. When you are finished, you are ready to start your new venture. Before you begin, let me show you how this can be done using the steps we have discussed in this book.

Let's start a business together. Did you read the first word in this paragraph? It means 'Let us." Instead of me telling you 'how to do it,' let us together build a business from the very beginning.

Peter and Paul

Our starting point on our grand adventure will be to discover how much money it takes to pay our monthly expenses and run our household. Then, we will compare our expenses with how much money we are currently earning each month. By subtracting our monthly expenses from our monthly income, we hopefully will come up with a positive number. If the result is a negative number, meaning were are spending more than we are earning, we either need to cut expenses somewhere or hurry and get our chosen business idea up and running as soon as possible to make up the difference.

Household Expenses

Expenses	Monthly Payment
Bank Charges	16.00
Cable TV	59.00
Cell Phone	55.00
Clothing	30.00
Credit Card Totals	280.00
Entertainment	200.00
Gasoline	180.00
Groceries	440.00
House Payment	1500.00
Internet	49.00
401(k) etc.	150.00
Medical Insurance	218.00
Postage	14.00
Vehicle Insurance	150.00
Vehicle Payment	325.00
Electric	95.00
Water	105.00
Gas	34.00
Sewer/Trash	33.00
Total Mo. Expenses	**3983.00**

This exercise now provides us with the dollar amount we will need to generate each month in our new venture. If you are currently working and receiving social security benefits, then your required monthly expenses may be less. If you are already retired and receiving social security benefits, hopefully you and your significant other's benefits combined are sufficient to make ends meet. If not, let's get this business up and going for additional cash flow.

Choosing A Business – The Idea

Next, let's decide what type of business we are going to create. After reviewing the 'List of Possible Start-Up Businesses' in Appendix B of this book, let's choose a pressure washing business. What can we do with a pressure washing business? We can clean residential concrete driveways as well as sidewalks and walkway entrances in front of stores and other businesses. We can clean the outside of mobile homes or trashcans at residential sites. We could even go to apartment complexes and clean up the trash that has spilled out over the top of the dumpsters and then wash out the area to minimize odors. Maybe someone needs their vehicle engine or other equipment cleaned. These are just some of the possibilities with this business.

Next, we will determine how much money it will take to begin this business enterprise using the 'Estimated Start-Up Costs' page, again from Appendix C. Here is what it looks like.

Appendix C
Estimated Start-Up Costs

Expense	Cost
Open Checking Account	100.00
Equipment	500.00
Fuel	75.00
Liability Insurance- Year	500.00
Licenses	100.00
Office Supplies	25.00
Permits	100.00
Printing	180.00

Vehicle Insurance	150.00
Vehicle Payment	325.00
Work Clothing	125.00
Est. Beginning Costs	**2235.00**

The 'equipment' column included your pressure washer, garden hose, ladder, gloves and other business related equipment to get you started. If some of these costs are more than you can afford at the moment, determine what you may be able to do without in the beginning. Remember, maybe someone you know already has these items and will let you borrow them for a period of time. Also, items such as cell phone, computer or office furniture were not included here. You probably already have these items and might be starting out in a spare bedroom or at the kitchen table.

What's in A Name?

Hey! Let's have some fun! What are we going to name our new business venture? Here is where we can get creative. Maybe we could call it 'Pressure Points Pressure Washing' or 'The Force Cleaning Systems,' 'Under Pressure Cleaning and Washing' or 'Strong Arm Pressure Cleaning.' For our business, I vote for Strong Arm Pressure Cleaning. A strong arm exudes strength and pressure cleaning tells people what it is we do.

We have performed our *due diligence* (homework.) We know how much it costs to run our life. We have chosen a particular business to start and we have given it a name. We also have a good idea of how much it is going to cost to get this venture up and running. Now we decide where we are going to get the money.

Start-Up Funding

After looking at our monthly budget, we determined that we are living paycheck to paycheck and have no other money to spare to start our new business. So, we got creative! We spoke with a family member and convinced them to loan us $500.00. We next had a garage sale and netted $800.00.

Fortunately, we were able to borrow $1200.00 from our 401(k) (which was about all we had in there.) We now have $2500.00 to begin our business venture. We owe $500.00 to a family member and $1200.00 to our company 401(k) plan, so we better make this new business work!

Business Structure

Since we are starting out by ourselves, we have elected to begin our business as a sole-proprietor. We went to the local government office and filed our *Fictitious Business Statement.*

This cost us $65.00. We next published our *Fictitious Business Statement* in a local legal newspaper. The cost was $50.00. Not long after, the legal newspaper sent us a copy of our published business name. We took a copy of our published Fictitious Business Statement and opened a business checking account known as Strong Arm Pressure Cleaning with $100.00 as our starting capital. We next went to our local city hall and applied for a city business license, which cost us $100.00. Wow! Our business is starting to take shape.

Create Our Image / Hook

Since the name of our company is ***Strong Arm Pressure Cleaning***, we came up with a logo of a strong arm raised to the square flexing it muscle. When people ask us what we do, we respond by saying *"I terrorize dirt with pressure and make things clean."* Next, we purchased two pair of coveralls for $60.00 and had our strong arm logo and company name embroidered on the front of each coverall for a total of $35.00.

Getting the Word Out

Next, we sat down at our computer and used Microsoft Publisher or Microsoft Power Point and designed a brochure to hand out to businesses and other potential clients. It didn't quite look right, so we asked a good friend who was good at graphic design to help us out. I'm glad we did. Our friend put together a 'killer' brochure and even designed some business cards for us. We couldn't afford to pay them, but found out they loved chocolate chip cookies. We baked five-dozen chocolate chip cookies and our friend was in heaven.

We took our new brochure design and went to a local copy store and for $11.00, made 100 copies to use for prospecting and advertising purposes. We also used our friend's graphic design and ordered a minimum of business cards from Vista Print on-line for $12.00.

We then went on-line to www.NEBS.com and chose and ordered service receipts and invoices for Strong Arm Pressure Cleaning. Our minimum order cost us $146.00 and arrived in about 9 days. While waiting for our invoices to arrive, we went to Wal-Mart and purchased a box of Number 10 business envelops, a clipboard and writing pens for $13.00.

Now comes our final step. After performing our *due diligence* and preparing our legal steps, we are now ready to use the larger portion of our seed money that has been held in reserve to purchase our large ticket items. We shopped around and found that Wal-Mart had a good intermediate pressure washer at a decent price. We also bought a garden hose, ladder, gloves, towels and other needed items. These all cost about $445.00. Then, just to be safe, we purchased a $500,000.00 business liability insurance policy to cover ourselves in case we damage property. This cost us $500.00 for the year.

Wow! Here we are. All our research and homework told us we would need $2235.00 to begin our new business. So far, we have spent $1537.00. We raised a total of $2500.00 from various sources. By subtracting the amount of money we have spent to get up and running of $1537.00 from our original starting capital of $2500.00, we have $963.00 left over as our working capital. **DO NOT** spend this money unless it is for a legitimate business purpose.

Promoting Your New Venture

You finally made it. You are now in business for yourself. What a marvelous feeling. You now have in your hands the opportunity to begin your trek towards financial freedom and security. Now it's time to let everyone know you are in business.

Are you on Facebook? Send out a message that you offer a valuable service. Take your brochures and business cards and walk in and lay a brochure on the desk of the apartment manager and tell them, "I just wanted to let you know that we are available to clean any areas of your property that might need a quick sprucing up. Thank you." Before leaving, ask the manager for their business card with a smile on your face. You now have a name and a number for contacting them again in the future. Do the same thing with property managers. They usually manage multiple office or residential properties. Also, as you drive down the street, be aware of the business and warehouse signs that show leasing opportunities. These signs will usually have a contact name and telephone number. Call and tell them what services you are offering and ask them for a mailing address to send them some information. Go visit a local mobile home park. They usually have a central community center with a bulletin board. If there is an on-site manager, ask permission to leave a brochure or business card on the bulletin board.

Remember social media. A simple website or constant tweets may be all it takes. Also look to 'gatekeepers' to help you. These are people who do similar business, but not exactly what you are doing. Network with them. Take them out to lunch or over coffee and a doughnut and discover how your business can complement their business.

Using your brochure, business card or a postcard you had printed, leave these on residential doorsteps offering your service to clean the grease and oil off their driveways or clean out their trashcans.

Please be aware that it is against federal postal laws to place anything in a mailbox. Penalties or fines can result.

Some Final Words

Do not expect any of the people you meet to engage your services immediately. You are laying the groundwork for possible future business. Most of the people you contact will not do business with you. But enough will do so to make it worth your while. Most businesses take time to build momentum. Be patient. If you currently have a job, continue working while promoting your new business (not at your job). If you are retired, then your full-time job is out prospecting and contacting people from 8:00am to 5:00pm. Prospecting is the hardest simple work to do. My experience is that it will not last long. Stay focused and out contacting people and businesses. Soon, you will no longer need to be out knocking on doors. People will be knocking on your door for service. Just keep on keeping on as the saying goes. You will be glad you did. *Don't ever be afraid to give up the good to get something better.*

[1] 177 Mental Toughness Secrets of the World Class, pg. 3, Steve Siebold, 2005

CHAPTER 15

Keeping Bread on the Table

"Sometimes, in business, you have to be a bit of a bastard."

- Famous rock star

Well, maybe not a (you know), but it can sometimes be aggravating to wait to get paid. You can work hard at your business all you want. But, until you get paid, nothing else matters. Always remember that **'cash flow is *more important* than profit'**. Cash flow helps you pay the bills. Cash flow is how you will pay your employees. Cash flow is how you purchase more inventory or supplies. It helps you keep your doors open *'one more day'*.

Each new start-up is usually starved for cash. When your customers do not pay you on time, you are essentially subsidizing their budgets. Is that why you want to go into business for yourself? Of course not!

Here are a few suggestions for keeping your cash flow coming in on a regular basis:

1. Make sure your clients know what your payment policy is right up front. You can verbally tell them or you can have it written into a contract, agreement or on a service slip. Tell your clients what services or products you will supply. Then, let them know that you expect to be paid in a reasonable amount of time. Usually 'net 30 days' if you have extended credit. Then, keep an eagle's eye on your receivables. (What you are owed.)

2. Offer a discount if they will pay you at the same time you provide your service. Usually 5%–10%.

3. Tell your clients they can deduct 5% from the amount owed if they will pay within 10 days of the date of the invoice. This is better than waiting the full 30 days. Be sure to watch out for those who may take advantage of this policy. Some clients will wait 25 days to pay and still deduct the 5%.

4. Let your clients know there will be a penalty for late payments. Maybe 2%–3% for every invoice over 30 days old. Check your local laws for limits than can be charged. Also, you will need to determine if chasing after the extra late payment penalty is worth it.

5. Offer your clients a discount when they refer a friend to your business.

6. Be sure to always keep in contact with your best clients. Send them a periodic thank you card expressing your appreciation for their business or timely payments. If a client is good at paying you and suddenly they get behind in their payment, give them a courtesy call and ask if everything is all right. Remember, 80% of your business typically comes from 20% of your clients. These are the clients you will want to spend the majority of your time serving.

I have found that being firm, but courteous usually gets me paid very quickly. On rare occasions, I have had to call the client and say, "I'm awfully sorry, but I won't be by next week because I haven't been paid as per our agreement." It has always amazed me how fast the client can get on the phone and get through to the accounts payable department. The check is often in the mail the same day. Keeping an eye on your business means keeping watch over your expenses as well as your income.

CHAPTER 16

Stupidity Kills

"Let's pass this bill so we can see what's in it."
Nancy Pelosi, House Leader
Affordable Healthcare Act Legislation 2010

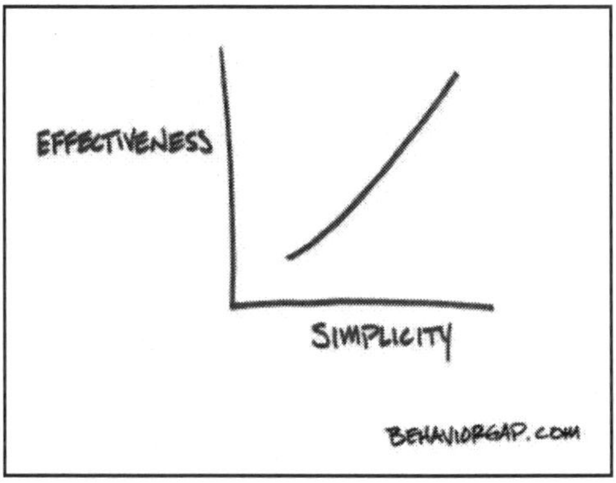

It's been said that most businesses fail due to a lack of money. I feel that's incorrect. Lack of money is a symptom of a larger problem. What kills most businesses is stupidity at the management level. Many business owners begin making some money and make the mistake of thinking this will continue day in and day out. So what do they do? Either they start spending the money on fun things, or they think they can take some time off and the money will continue to roll in. The reality is that a start-up takes a lot of hard work, determination, perseverance and keeping an eye on things before it can run on autopilot. It also takes time to build. Cash flow is a fluid commodity. Some days you earn more money than other days. The amount of money coming in on a daily basis also varies day to day. Some days you collect a lot of money and other days no money comes in at all. It's an up and down reality. Problem is, the bills and expenses continue to roll in. You need to keep the pipeline filled with work and effort if you want cash flow to come out at the other end of the pipeline on a regular schedule.

I was once involved with a company that designed and manufactured intra-oral video cameras for the dental industry. You know, those little cameras the dentist puts in your mouth to make that little crack in your back molar appear like the Grand Canyon on the video monitor? I was involved as the senior VP from the very beginning. We first had an idea. Then we researched the marketplace and found a need. We found an 'Angel' for our financing. Then, we searched for parts and equipment and began the design and manufacturing process. Sales soon began going through the roof. We started out in a garage and finally graduated to an office and small assembly room. We were having fun and making a lot of money. Then, a very interesting phenomenon occurred. The owner of the company began to have visions of grandeur and rented a spacious building full of plush offices, a lunchroom, assembly area, conference room and a grand suite for his office. The expenses started to grow and the mood in the building changed. Instead of having fun and making money, we were constantly being reminded that we had expenses and that we needed to increase our sales. The pressure started to mount. Then came the death knell.

The company owner decided to bring his three daughters into the business. Suddenly, there were three *'supervisors'* watching everything we were doing. They reported back to daddy that we were *only* working 9-10 hours a day and we were *only* bringing in about $30,000.00 each per week in sales. The three daughters began protecting daddy and everyone else became the enemy. Needless to say, after trying my best to keep the company afloat, it failed less than 10 months after my departure.

Keep your eyes on the goal of building a business that one day will run itself without you having to be there. Stay true to your core business and don't try to take on too much or go in too many directions. **Remember, stupidity kills! Keep it simple.**

CHAPTER 17

A Final Word About "YOU"

World-Class Freedom Begins with World-Class Thinking

G. Edward Marshall

A Final Note

When beginning your own business, if you haven't already, you will want to begin forging relationships with CPAs, bankers, insurance brokers, printers, suppliers and other 'gatekeepers.' Napoleon Hill calls this your 'Mastermind Group.' These are people who have specialized knowledge about things you don't know or don't have time to learn. They can be very helpful and will usually cost less to use them than the cost of the mistakes you may incur on your own. Look to people you know and how you can help others increase their business. If done correctly, they will in turn send clients to you.

Are there downsides to being a business owner? Absolutely. You may have limited time to see your friends or other family members as you build your business. However, after your business is built and eventually on autopilot, you can turn around and help your friends and family much more than you ever could have before. As a retiree and a business owner, you decide when to work and when to play. You've earned the right to control your destiny. By growing a business of your own, you can create a golden goose that can provide you with golden eggs to pursue your dreams. Go forward. Follow your dream, and make mistakes and gain wisdom and experience. Next time around you'll know the right course of action to take. Isn't that what regular life is about anyway? You might as well start your own business instead of getting a job and building someone else's dream. Succeed modestly or greatly. Either way, you're succeeding.

When you first begin your business, take any job or contract you can. Cash flow is king. As was mentioned before, cash flow is often more important than profit. You heard me. Why? Because cash flow keeps your company doors open one more day.

In your new venture, just continue pressing forward. Even when you don't want to, just keep working. For every action, there is an opposite and equal reaction. One of these days, you are going to wake up and you may have more work and customers to take care of than you have time for. Won't that be cool? It's your business. You can stay busy or you can slow things down. Persevere and it will all be worth it. I know! I've been there and it works!

Most people wait until all their ducks are lined up in a row. Don't wait. Most people say "Ready, aim, fire!" If you do, you will never get started. Trust me. I've tried doing that. It doesn't work. Don't wait to begin. ***Ready, fire, aim*** is the way to go. As a businessperson in my late sixties, I have learned that you can usually get more money, but you cannot get more time. That's why I believe in ***Ready, FIRE, aim.***

Give your new venture at least six months. If it's not working out, re-evaluate what you are doing. By following the principles outlined in this book, I promise you will make fewer mistakes and get to your desired destination faster and with fewer headaches.

Increased cash flow improves the quality of your life and affords additional vacations. This is what being a business owner can provide. When beginning a new business venture, I again implore you to start with the goal of building a business and **hiring others to run it for you as soon as possible. Then, you can leave and go do the really important things in life.** Did you understand what I just said? Again, go back and re-read that previous line again. It took me way too long to learn this concept.

I also want you to remember the last four letters in the word enthusiasm. They stand for "I am sold myself." Be the best you can be. Really believe in what you do. Solve people's problems. I have learned that rather than out looking for success, it's better to attract success. Be the successful person you know you can be and people will seek you out and pay you to solve their problems. If you don't want to start a full-time business at first, begin part-time selling popcorn, balloons or providing a service. Earn some extra money.

Remember your 'Golden Hours.' These are the times during the day or night that you concentrate on working. These are your most profitable times of the day or night where you can earn income for your business. Run your errands before or after work hours. As you fill the pipeline with work, eventually, revenue comes pouring out the other end. Don't let anything interfere with your 'Golden Hours.' Again, you are building the golden goose in your business so that eventually you can live off the golden eggs. Eventually, you will have enough customers to keep all of your employees busy so you no longer have to 'work' for your daily upkeep. You can live on the golden eggs (income) your venture produces each month. Just be sure to keep an eye on the goose.

Before we close, I want to ask you one last question. "Are you relying on one source of income?" You may already be receiving social security benefits each month. You may also have some savings or a 401(k), IRA or annuity you can draw upon. If you have any of the latter, good for you. However, I have found that relying on one source of income can be a dangerous way to live. All your eggs are in one basket. Look at all the people who had a job during the

Coronavirus pandemic. Many people were told to go home and come back when things improve. The problem was, many didn't get paid while they went home to wait it out. This is why I believe it is a GREAT idea to have *'multiple streams of income.'* Think of a pedestal table. It has one large pedestal to hold the table upright. If something were to happen to the pedestal, the entire table becomes unstable or falls apart. Now, think of a picnic table. It has two benches and four legs to support it. If one of the legs or a bench are damaged or removed, the table may wobble, but it is still able to stand. Think of the table as your life and each of the legs as one of your income streams. Having more than one income stream reduces the threat of a financial disaster.

Follow my counsel and start your business as soon as possible. You will later ask yourself why you waited so long. I am now better off financially ***because*** I am in business for myself. Remember that 'Entrepreneurship' is living a few years of your life like most people won't, so you can spend the rest of your life living like most people can't. **Create Income 2 Retire** and live out your remaining years with dignity and enjoyment.

G. Edward Marshall

APPENDIX A

Estimated Household Expenses

Download this form at www.CreateIncome2Retire.com

EXPENSES	Monthly Payment
Bank Charges	
Cable TV	
Cell Phone	
Charity	
Clothing	
Credit Card Totals	
Entertainment	
Gasoline	
Groceries	
House Payment 1st	
House Payment 2nd	
HELOC	
House Insurance	
Internet	
401k, etc.	
Life Insurance	
Medical Expense	
Dental Expense	
Postage	
Savings	
Subscriptions	
House Phone	
Car Insurance	
Car Maintenance	
Vehicle Pmt. #1	

Vehicle Pmt. #2	
Other:	
Other:	
Other:	
Electric	
Water	
Gas	
Trash/Sewer	
Total Mo. Expenses	

APPENDIX B

Partial List of Possible Start-Up Businesses

Download this form at www.CreateIncome2Retire.com

3-D Printer Service
Accountant
Adult Daycare
Advertising
Air Conditioning
Antique Dealer
Appraiser
Arborist
Architect
Artist/Artist Supply
Auctioneer
Audio/Visual Service
Auditor
Auto Detail
Auto Mechanic
Bakery
Beauty Salon/Supply
Beverage Distributor
Bodyguard Service
Candy Maker/Store
Carpenter
Carpet/Flooring
Carpet Cleaning
Catering Service
Check Cashing
Childcare/After School
Clothing Store Owner
Coffee Delivery Service
Computer Consultant
Computer Repair
Contract Writer
Consultant Delivery Service
Designer
Diesel Repair
Direct Mail Service
Donut Store
Drywall Repair
Electrician
Employment Agency
Engineer
Errand Service
Farmer
Flood/Fire Repair
Florist
Foreclosures
Franchise Owner
Fund Raiser
General Contracting

Granite Countertops
Graphic Design
Grocery Store
Handyman
Health Care
Heating & Cooling
Home Healthcare
Home Inspection
House Cleaning/Sanitizing
House Sitter
Import-Export
Insurance Agent
Interior Decorator
Janitorial Service
Janitorial Supply
Jewelry Repair/Sales
Laundromat
Landscaping
Lawn Care
Lawn Fertilizing
Lecturer
Limousine Service
Long-Term Care
Machinist
Magnetic Sign Service
Management Consultant
Marketing Service
Medical Transportation
Mobile Home Repair
Mobile Income Tax
Moving & Storage
Music Teacher
Networks Specialist
Newsletter Writer
Notary
Office Machines
Office Supply
Painting
Party Planner
Pest Control
Pet Sitting
Petting Zoo
Photographer
Pilot Car Service
Pizza Restaurant
Plumbing
Pool Cleaning/Repair
Pooper Scooper
PO Box Store
Pressure Washing
Printing Service
Private Tutor
Property Manager
Public Relations
Publisher
Real Estate Agent
Roofing Contracting
Sales Rep
Salvage/Scrap Metal
Sand Blasting

Sandwich/Deli Store
Santa Claus
Screen Printing
Screen Repair Service
Security Service
Service Station Owner
Ship/Boat Repair/Sales
Sign Maker/Service
Smart Phone Tutor
Social Media
Tax Preparation
Tool Supply
Trash Can Cleaning
Travel Agency
Tree Trimming
Used Car Sales
Vehicle Parts Store
Water Delivery Service
Wedding Planner
Welding Contracting
Welding Supply
Wholesale Distributor
Window/Glass Repair
Window Washing
Yard Clean Up

APPENDIX C

Estimated Start-Up Costs

Download this form at www.CreateIncome2Retire.com

Expense	Cost
Advertising	
Bank Charges	
Cell Phone	
Credit Cards	
Dues	
Estimated Quarterly Taxes	
Fuel	
Gifts Given	
Legal Fees	
Licenses	
Permits	
Liability Insurance	
Vehicle Insurance	
Vehicle Payment	
Vehicle Maintenance	
Office Supplies	
Office Equipment	
Office Furniture	
Office Rent	
Postage	
Printing	
Fax Line	
Internet	
Work Clothing	
Utilities	

Subscriptions	
Payroll	
Payroll Taxes	
Workmen's Comp Insurance	
Toll Lane Fees	
Other	
Other	
Total Beginning Fees	

APPENDIX D

The Start-Up Checklist

THE BEGINNING

- ❑ Decided Upon You 'WHY'
- ❑ Belief in Yourself
- ❑ Positive Attitude
- ❑ Estimated Personal Monthly Expenses

STEP ONE

- ❑ You Chosen Idea
- ❑ Estimated Start-Up Expenses
- ❑ A mentor / Franchise / Friendly & Supportive Resource

STEP TWO

- ❑ Company Name

STEP THREE

- ❑ Finding Start-Up Capital

STEP FOUR

__ Sole Proprietorship
__ Partnership
__ C-Corp
__ S-Corp
__ LLC

- ❑ Filed Your Legal Name

__ Fictitious Business Name Statement)Sole Prop, Partnership, LLC)

__ Articles of Incorporation (C or S Corp)

- ❑ Publish Your Legal Name

STEP FIVE

- ❑ Created Your Image / Hook
- ❑ Uniform

STEP SIX

- ❑ Business Telephone
- ❑ Business Checking Account
- ❑ Banking Software To Track Income & Expenses
- ❑ Licenses
- ❑ Permits
- ❑ Insurance
  - __ Business Liability
  - __ Bond
  - __ Workmen's Comp
  - __ Vehicle Insurance

STEP SEVEN

- ❑ Advertising
  - __ Business Cards
  - __ Sales/Service Receipts
  - __ Invoices
  - __ Envelops
  - __ Brochure/Post Card

STEP EIGHT

- ❑ Equipment
- ❑ Product
- ❑ Vehicle

- ❑ Home Office / Office / Warehouse
  - __ Sign
  - __ Office Equipment
  - __ Office Supplies

STEP NINE

- ❑ Client Account Software For Billing And Payments

STEP TEN

- ❑ Opened An Account With A Supplier
- ❑ Joined a Networking Group

STEP ELEVEN

- ❑ Website
- ❑ Employer Identification Number (EIN) (For hiring employees) (IRS)
- ❑ Payroll Service
- ❑ Hire the Right People
- ❑ Trained Employees Properly

APPNEDIX E

A Partial List of Available Tax Deductionss

Download this form at www.CreateIncome2Retire.com

Advertising
Alarm Systems
Bank Fees
Business Cards
Business Bond
Business Brochures
Business Insurance
Business License
Business Lunches
Business Training
Cell Phone
Checking Account Fees
Computer
Computer Repait
Computer Software
Copy Machine
Charity
Clothing
Consulting Fees
Continuing Education
Desk
Dry Cleaning
Enterraining
E & O Insurance
Fax Machine
Filing Cabinet
Gasoline
Gifts Given
Health Insurance
Inkjet Cartridges
Internet
Inventory Supplies
Legal Fees
License Fees
Mortgage Payment
Office Cleaning
Office Rent
Office Supplies
Office Equipment
Office Furniture
Office Utilities
Paper
Payroll
Postage
Printing
Printer
Printing Supplies
Parts
Rent Payment
Shipping Charges

Stamps
Subscriptions
Telephone
Telephone System
Thank You Cards
Toll Lanes
Tools
Uniforms
Utilities
Vehicle Payment
Vehicle Insurance
Vehicle Maintenance
Vehicles Mileage
Website Fee

- Only a portion of these expenses may be deducted. Seek professional advice.

ABOUT THE AUTHOR

G. Edward Marshall was born and raised in Long Beach, CA. He spent two years as a Christian missionary in southern Japan. Mr. Marshall has travelled the world and interviewed many business owners. He has worked as a delivery driver, an outside sales representative, a pest control company owner, a dental camera inventor, a Japanese Joint Venture Specialist and in financial services. He has also served in multiple leadership positions in several civic organizations. His passion is helping people start businesses, create additional income, reduce their taxes and live a more financially fulfilling life. He and his wife Debbie have been married for more than 46 years. They have four children and enjoy spending time with their eight grandchildren.

For more information or to download worksheets:
www.CreateIncome2Retire.com

We would love to hear from you.
Your comments are always welcome.
CreateIncome2Retire@gmail.com

ACKNOWLEDGEMENTS

I would like to give a world of thanks to some special people in my life. To Russell Hardy who has been by my side for so many years and seems almost like a brother to me. To my good friend Paul Berney who has been a source of constant support and encouragement. To my best friend, confidant and wife Debbie who has stayed with me through both the good and the tough times and continues to be my biggest cheerleader in life.

A special thank you to Dawn Andrews at Mental Toughness University for allowing me to use some great quotes from Steve Siebold's book, "177 Mental Toughness Secrets of the World Class." Also, to Darren Scott at HardPress Publishing for copyright use of "Bunker Bean." A special thank you to Larry Brock, Esq., for his proofreading and positive critique of my original manuscript.

1 Reason to Read This Book Just for Baby Boomers!

Is your retirement where rocking horse people eat marshmallow pies with tangerine trees and marmalade skies? Or, do you need a little help from your friends? Was your 401(k) eight miles high and then the stock market took it away? Twice? Hey! We're baby boomers, we can work it out.

Ever thought about being your own boss? My new book "Create Income 2 Retire" will teach you how to start and build a cash-flow business of your own in retirement. Money may not buy you love, but it can put you in a great bargaining position. Starting a business is no magical mystery tour. This book is easy to follow and will guide you step-by-step.

For the price of a latte and a happy meal, you can have what you need to be free from the purple haze of struggling along and let happy days smile again on you.

Get this book or download it today to your smart phone, I-Pad, Kindle or e-book reader. Sorry, 8-track and vinyl albums are no longer available. Still working for the weekend, but just can't get no satisfaction? Replace income with a business of your own and live your 'Golden Years' in dignity.

Here is the answer to your retirement income concerns. When you're 64 and down to your last dollar, it really can be the loneliest number. Get this book now!

Made in the USA
Columbia, SC
11 October 2020

22603737R00065